Coming For You
A Contemporary Romance Novella

PAM KELLY

COMING FOR YOU

This book is a work of fiction. Names, characters, businesses, organizations, places, events, and incidents either are the product of the author's research or imagination or are used fictitiously. Any resemblance to actual persons, living or dead, or events, is entirely coincidental.

Copyright © 2025 by Pamela F. Kelly

All rights reserved. The reproduction, transmission, or utilization of this work, in whole or in part, in any form by electronic, mechanical, or other means, now known or hereafter invented, including xerography, photocopying, or recording, or in any information storage or retrieval system, except brief quotes used in reviews, is forbidden without written permission. For permission, please contact Pam Kelly: Pam@AuthorPamKelly.com

ISBN: 978-0-9801502-7-8 (paperback)
ISBN: 978-0-9801502-8-5 (ebook)

Editor: Katara Patton
Cover Design: Joseph John / Print-O-Graph of America
Formatting: Word-2-Kindle

Also by PAM KELLY:

LEAP OF FAITH
A Romance Novel

VALENTINE LOVE

"Love recognizes no barriers. It jumps hurdles, leaps fences, penetrates walls to arrive at its destination full of hope."

Maya Angelou

IN LOVING MEMORY OF MY SISTER
ADRIAN CECILIA KERSH FLEMING
She was love personified to all who knew her,
and she had her own one-of-a-kind love story
that I was honored to witness.

Chapter One

She knew she was being watched. People at the apartment building where she lived always spoke to each other the way that people in the South were known to do whether they knew each other or not – with a quick "Hello!" or a nod or a wave.

Lisa Price had moved to the building late in December, and in the New Year, she had become a familiar, friendly face to others who lived there.

Lisa considered herself an introvert, quiet but always showing a pleasant expression on her face, easy to approach and engage in conversation. She was good at getting other people to talk about themselves while sharing very little about herself. She was not hiding anything from people, she was just a private person. Besides, most people loved to talk about themselves, so it was easy to get them to do so.

She usually saw the same people when she was leaving or returning home, and the greetings to her had progressed to conversations that included compliments on her red Jaguar, how nicely she was dressed every time she went out, and her neighbors sharing information on how long they had lived in the building, their jobs, their families, and even gossip about other tenants. She enjoyed getting to know them.

The Thompson family was particularly friendly towards her. Ruth Thompson was the 90-year-old matriarch of the family. She was a 5' 10" tall, statuesque woman, with smooth dark chocolate skin and short cut, silky, curly white hair. She was mother to two sons, Roman and Quincy, both of whom, she was proud to say, looked just like her. She was the beloved grandmother or "G" to Roman's two sons, Eli and Danny.

Ms. Ruth was a widow who, for years lived with her oldest son, Roman, to help raise his two boys. She never explained why that was necessary and Lisa did not ask, believing that she would eventually find out.

Now Ms. Ruth lived on the first floor of the same building Lisa lived in, with Quincy, her youngest son. Like his mom, Quincy was tall (6 feet) and dark chocolate, but bald. He was a semi-retired chef who helped his friends in the industry with large events, special occasions, and in an emergency, a shift at their restaurants.

Divorced with no children, Quincy became the designated caregiver for Ms. Ruth after the boys graduated high school and she moved out of Roman's house.

The mother and son's apartment patio faced the parking lot so in good weather, they sat outside people watching and relaxing. They were the first people in the building who waved and called out, "Good morning" and "Happy New Year" to Lisa.

In the evenings, they called her over to chat about family, TV shows and movies, and especially cooking and recipes when they found out that they all shared the same passion for food. This often led to Quincy asking her to try something he had cooked for family night. Thursday was when Ms. Ruth insisted Roman, Eli, and Danny come for dinner and hang out with her each week, watching game shows or murder mysteries, or playing table games.

After about a month of chatting on the patio and taste testing, Lisa was invited to join them for dinner each Thursday so she could meet Eli, Danny, and eventually, Roman. Roman was often absent because of work.

Lisa met Eli and Danny in mid-February, on the first Thursday she agreed to have dinner with the Thompson family. They were graduate students and wrote poetry, making appearances at poetry slams about once a month.

"I want to be like my dad and work for a large manufacturing company, figuring out how to get new products through production and out to consumers. My degree will be in Production Management." Eli looked like the pictures of Roman, with the same dark coloring and facial features.

Danny had a lighter, more caramel colored skin tone, and curly brown hair. Lisa assumed he looked more like his mom. "I want to help create policies and programs for people with health problems to get medicine at lower costs and in-home services that could help keep them out of hospitals and nursing homes. My degree will be a Master of Science in Social Policy."

Both young men were immediately taken with Lisa, thinking she was pretty and kind. She seemed genuinely interested in their activities, not phony as she asked questions to get to know them. They invited her to their next poetry night at Sugar's. She went and had a great time with them.

Lisa had seen many pictures of Roman on the long wall of family photos as she entered the Thompson apartment; from naked baby to scrawny kid to gym rat muscle building teen and young adult, to today's six-foot, deep brown smooth chocolate, very toned manly man.

There was no doubt that Roman was handsome. Her breath caught in her throat every time she looked at his pictures. She was captivated by his almond shaped eyes. His direct look into the camera made her feel like he could see her looking at his pictures. His sexy smile made her feel like he was happy to see her looking at him.

Eli described Roman to her. "Pops is usually in a good mood. We spend a lot of time together when his schedule allows, and we laugh a lot. Then he has his serious side, very dedicated to his work and always caring for us to make sure we are okay and have what we need."

But nothing prepared her for actually meeting Roman in person.

It was a Thursday evening, family night. She was on the elevator, headed down from her second floor apartment, to the Thompson apartment on the first floor. When the door to the elevator opened, there he was.

He was about to walk past, but when the elevator door opened, he turned to look to see who was inside. He saw Lisa, stopped dead in his tracks, then turned to face her. They stared at each other as he held the door open. He did not try to hide the way he looked at her from head to toe and back again. She looked at him the same way.

Lisa knew who he was and was overwhelmed. He reminded her of an African warrior with his imposing stature, calm and calculating presence, confidence, and class. She could feel the sweat break out on her body and it took everything she had to hold on to the pan of hot peach cobbler in the carrier that she held in her hands.

He was attracted to the woman he saw. She was beautiful, with thick, natural, salt and pepper, short cut hair, a pointy nose, and a sexy heart-shaped mouth. She was dressed very simply in jeans, a long sleeved blouse with the sleeves rolled up, and a pair of ballet flats.

What captured his attention was that she had an ethereal presence about her, a glow surrounding her that made her look poised and confident, yet soft and yielding. She looked like a woman who knew who she was and what she wanted and would not be easily impressed so she would not share herself too quickly.

He felt an immediate connection to her.

They had a moment. The attraction was instant and mutual and they both knew in their spirit that their lives were destined to be connected forever. It was the knowing that excited him and frightened her.

Chapter Two

Eli and Danny walked into the lobby talking and bumped into Roman, not realizing he had stopped at the elevator. When they looked inside and saw Lisa, they both greeted her with excitement.

"Hey Ms. Lisa! Is that dessert for us? We will take that."

When the boys said her name, a huge grin spread across Roman's face.

"Well, well. I finally get to meet the fabulous Lisa Price. In person. Hello." His voice was deep and smooth, gently caressing her ears.

She responded in kind. "Hello Roman. It's nice to finally meet the legend in the flesh."

He followed her to his Mom's apartment. Everybody was excited that Lisa and Roman had finally met after two months of her getting to know the rest of the family.

When he first heard about Lisa, Roman was happy his Mom had a new friend. Initially, he thought Lisa was his mother's age. When they told him that Lisa was around his and Quincy's age, he became suspicious. There were many stories about women who befriended older people then swindled them out of money and other valuables. The more he learned though, the more interested he became in meeting her. He decided that if she could win over his whole family, she must be special. He was quickly learning why.

They spent the evening telling stories of how Lisa became special to the family.

His sons were enamored with her. They came home the first day they met her talking about how great she was, and had been very complimentary every week since.

Danny spoke first. "She is so cool Pops, asking us about school and our classes, and about our perspective on politics and social media and people. When we told her about the women we are dating, she asked what we were doing to court them, and what kind of relationships we wanted. We love hearing her thoughts and ideas on romance, including where we go on dates that don't cost a lot of money since we are in school.

Then Eli chimed in. "She even asked about how we came up with our poetry and she came to Sugar's to hear us when you were out of town. She is the one who encouraged us to learn a new vocabulary word every week; to help us in business as well as in writing poetry. Now you know she cooks some great desserts! You've been missing out."

His brother, Quincy, loved Lisa for his own reasons.

"She is a diabetes management expert so she knows about foods to eat and those to avoid, and portion control. Mom and I are both pre-diabetic so the healthy eating tips she gives us are very helpful.

"Not only that, she collects recipes and does not mind sharing them. She has recipes for all kinds of meat, vegetables, and pastas. She has a particular interest in spices to change up the flavor of a dish so you are never bored with it. I am trying something new every month because of her.

"We have a routine now too. I cook the meals for family night, she brings dessert because that is her specialty, but she makes them in a healthy way. She also comes to dinner every now and then after church on Sundays when it's just me and Mom."

His Mom loved having the female companionship, a daughter even.

"I'm old, so most of my lady friends are gone. It's nice to have a woman to talk to instead of all you boys. We even did manicures and pedicures together for Valentine's Day. It's as if I have a daughter now. Don't get me wrong, I love all of you, but it's nice to have a female to talk to."

They had already added Lisa to the family text chat so she could be a part of their news and updates.

Throughout dinner and the rest of the evening, Roman watched Lisa as they told more stories, listened to her respond to his family, and noticed that she was avoiding looking at him or talking directly to him. He smiled because he believed that meant she was attracted to him but she was fighting it. He couldn't figure out why so it piqued his curiosity.

Chapter Three

Roman came to the family dinner the next Thursday, hoping to see Lisa again and find a way to talk to her without his family around before he had to go out of town again. She was polite, but mostly ignored him like she had done the previous week. He was disappointed, but knew their time would come.

After Lisa left, Roman told Quincy about the moment in the elevator when he first saw Lisa, and how attracted to her he was.

Quincy usually didn't interfere in his brother's private life, but this time was an exception.

"You know we all like her man. What you may not know is that we all think she would be great for you."

Roman was puzzled. "Why don't you want to be with her? You see her all the time and you seem to get along well."

"We do, but she's like a sister to me, has been from day one. I want her for a sister-in-law though. And Eli and Danny are hoping that you two would connect and she would join the family, be their mother, even at this stage of their lives."

Roman was intrigued. He had not dated anyone special in years and to hear that they all thought she would be good for him made him think more about her. He was gone all of the next week, returning late on Friday. He thought of Lisa every day and the possibilities of her being that special someone in his life.

On Saturday, after he got back, he stopped by in the afternoon to drop off some medicine for his Mom. He and Ms. Ruth were sitting on the patio when Lisa drove up and opened her trunk. It was full of groceries.

Roman insisted on helping her get the bags and case of water to her apartment. He finally had the opportunity he wanted to speak with her alone. She did not refuse him but was nervous about what he would say to her.

"Nice place Ms. Lisa Price," he said as he entered her apartment. He noticed soft music playing when they walked in and the scent was light and feminine. Her furnishings were a stark contrast to her conservative, neutral attire—a bright azure blue sofa and two butter yellow woven leather chairs, lots of glass tables and glass accessories, thick multi-colored area rugs that tied in the colors of the sofa and chairs. Her artwork was mainly colorful paintings of people. He wanted to take his shoes off and make himself at home. He set the grocery bags down on the counter and put the case of water on the floor where she pointed.

"Thanks. And thanks for helping me with the bags too." She was about to walk in front of him to lead him to the door so he would leave but he started taking items out of the bags and handing them to her.

"I can do that. I'm sure you have better things to do with your Saturday afternoon."

"Actually there is nowhere else I would rather be right now than here with you. I have heard so much about you and after seeing you myself, I know exactly why you have captivated everyone in the Thompson family. I'm now part of your fan club too." He smiled at her, but she was putting canned goods in the cabinet and did not see the look.

She avoided looking at him whenever they were in the same space. He was so handsome to her she would begin to sweat every time he was around. Her breathing became labored so she could hardly speak. Apparently, he had noticed that she became flushed when he was around.

When the groceries were put away, he took the opportunity to engage her again. "Ms. Lisa, may I ask you a question?"

"Sure." She was trying to ignore him by folding bags and putting them in the pantry.

"Why don't you look at me?"

"What do you mean? I do look at you," she replied, without looking at him.

"No, I've watched you and you always look over my shoulder or at someone else. Why is that?"

She knew she was busted but she still tried to give an excuse. "I look at you but usually when you are not looking at me."

"Well that can't be often because I'm staring at you every time we are in the same room, trying to get your attention. Don't you feel the heat seeking missiles I've been shooting at you?"

She smiled but turned to put bottles of water in the refrigerator to avoid looking at him.

"That's what you call the looks—heat seeking missiles?" She shook her head. "Yes, I feel them."

"Then you know that I am attracted to you. And if you are feeling them, I would say you are attracted to me too. I want to ask you out so we can get to know each other without the family around."

They were both quiet. He was looking at her, enjoying the view and waiting for her response. She finally looked directly at him, trying to figure out how to say no and mean it. He was very handsome and sexy, but she had to say no.

Finally, he said, "So, will you go out with me?"

"No, thanks," she replied quietly.

"Why not?" He was perplexed. In his mind, both were single adults and attracted to each other. What was the problem?

She stopped pretending to be busy and nodded for him to follow her to the family room to sit. In her mind, she wanted to be honest so that he would not think she was being rude but would understand and not pursue her.

She sat on the sofa and he pulled up a chair in front of her. As he sat, he made sure their knees touched. He leaned over and took her hands in his, rubbing her palms with his thumbs, creating a flow of heat from her hands, up her arms, and down to her toes.

"Talk to me."

Lisa took a deep breath, looked up to his handsome face and into his eyes. He was looking at her with a curious expression, eager to hear what she had to say.

Chapter Four

"I don't look at you a lot because you make me nervous, anxious really. Sweat breaks out on my face, arms, and hands, and I can't catch my breath. You give me the vapors. That is not a good sign." She pauses to shake her head and smile.

"You were probably one of the 'pretty boys' back in the day. I've dated handsome men like you before. I have a strong attraction to your type, and it makes me all giddy and excited, but it never turns out well.

"In the past, the pretty boys thought I was weak for them and cheated on me, or they did other things that hurt me. I am too old for that now, so I avoid relationships with men who make me feel that way. They are trouble with a capital T.

"You are a handsome, charismatic man. I've heard that you have several women in your life so I can't figure out why you need to add me to the group. I don't fit your preferred profile, and I'm not interested in being an experiment for you."

"I have a preferred profile?" he asked, surprised at her assessment.

"Yes. I have seen your high school prom and your wedding pictures. The young lady and your wife could be the same person they look so similar. You like tall, very thin, light if not white women with long flowing hair. The model type. I am none of those, given that I am average height, definitely not thin, and I do not wear weaves or wigs. I'm not sure why you're acting as if you are interested.

"I am not about to go out with you because we had a moment at the elevator and now you want to try someone new.

"Furthermore, I will not date you just because your family likes me. The truth is I don't want to date you because when it's time to move on, it will make things uncomfortable for me with your family. I cannot have that. I really like them. I see them so often they are like family to me now and you cannot mess that up for me.

"Besides, I have a good man that I am dating, and one man is enough for me."

She paused to gauge his reaction. He was looking at her with a scowl on his face, waiting to see if there was more. There was.

"There is one final issue that I have. Your family living here gives you direct access to my place. I don't want to be with a man who can be all up in my life that way, anytime, unexpectedly.

"So, thanks for asking, but I'm good just knowing you and seeing you when I see you with your family."

Lisa stopped talking but kept looking in his eyes, feeling triumphant that she had given him all of her reasons and was strong in her conviction that she would not date him and maybe could now look at him without becoming a muddled mess.

Roman had a questioning look on his face, which prompted him to ask, "What in the world are the vapors?"

Lisa smiled again.

"As I said, you make me anxious, sweaty, breathless. My grandmother used to tell me stories of how, back in her day, women who felt faint or were swooning when men they liked came around to court them, were considered to have the vapors."

Roman slowly nodded, and Lisa could see he was thinking, processing all that she had said.

She was thinking to herself that she had to get him out of her apartment quickly because he was looking at her with such interest and concern, he smelled good, and he never stopped rubbing her palms. She only had so much will power.

Lisa pulled her hands back then pushed his legs away so she could stand and walk him to the door.

"Thanks again for your help with the groceries. I'll see you another time."

Roman paused at the door. "That was a lot to unpack Ms. Lisa. I don't get to respond? To offer a different point of view?"

"No need. I am not changing my mind. Like I said, been there, done that. I'm good without it." Lisa believed that she had cleared the air with Roman so the vapors would not be an issue anymore.

Roman wanted to press her against the wall and kiss her until she changed her mind but he knew he had to proceed gently with her.

"Thank you for your honesty. I will see you again. Have a good night." He walked slowly toward the elevator knowing he had to decide if he could eliminate all of her reasons for not dating him.

He knew already, from what his family said about her and now what he had seen for himself, that she was worth whatever he had to do to spend time with her.

Chapter Five

She was right, she looked nothing like most of the women he had dated, but it was because he mostly dated the women who came on to him. Men can sometimes be lazy, and with all that he had on his plate, he was lackadaisical about seeking women.

He was all for changing up though, especially for this woman who was so appealing to him. She was classy, elegant in the casual confident way she carried herself, and she didn't seem snobby. She was beautiful with pretty eyes, a killer smile, and a very sexy body.

Roman studied Lisa closely, and could tell she was intelligent based on the types of questions she asked Danny and Eli about their classes and the insightful comments she made when they talked about world news. He even liked her smart assessments of "who done it" when watching his Mom's favorite murder mystery shows.

She seemed serious much of the time, but had a great sense of humor, laughing at jokes and teasing with the family members as she got to know them. It was definitely a bonus that his family already adored her.

Roman made a brief stop to say good-bye to his Mom and brother and head home. They could tell from the look on his face that he was in deep thought. His mother asked, "Are you ok? What happened with Lisa?"

"I'm not okay, Mom. She gave me a list of reasons why she would not date me. A LIST. What can I do with a list?" His Mom and brother looked at each other and smiled, both thinking Lisa would give him a run for his money if they did go out.

"Well brother," Quincy commented. "You will figure it out. Or better yet, just leave her alone. You don't stick with women too long and we don't need you coming in here and messing up our relationship with her. Stay with those lightweights you usually sneak around with and keep away from us." Quincy knew Roman well and their Mom nodded her head in agreement.

Roman drove home slowly, then he couldn't sleep all night. He had never been so summarily rejected by someone who admitted to the mutual attraction. He didn't want to override her objections just because his ego was bruised. He had already decided that if he could get to know more about her, she could possibly be someone he could date exclusively, something he had not done since his first son, Eli, was a toddler over twenty years ago.

Maybe she would be interested in the long-term relationship that he wanted.

He had made it a point to go to dinner on the Thursday they met. She was everything they said. He also saw in her a sexy, confident woman who was very private because she always asked the family questions but shared very little about herself. He was intrigued and eager to get to know the personal side of her.

The question was how could he even begin the uphill climb to get with her? For work, he developed feasibility studies on how to fit new products into current production systems, which included trouble shooting and problem solving. He realized he would have to use that same skillset to strategize on Ms. Lisa Price.

Chapter Six

Lisa was up all night too. She had not been attracted to a man like Roman in a long time and it was hard to say no to him. Nevertheless, she had to. She did not want to end up like her mother.

Her dad was very handsome and had a big personality that attracted people, especially women. He loved the attention and had cheated on her mother for years. Her mother knew and was devastated but stayed with him because she loved him. Lisa could feel her pain and swore she would never love a man like that. Yet her choices in relationships in earlier years led her to the fun pretty boys and the heartache they brought with them. Therapists have said that women are often subconsciously looking for their father in a man, even a father who is a bad example.

Lisa had been rejected in high school by a very handsome young man when she was supposed to go to her prom, then his, the same year. They went to hers. Then he called three days before his prom to say he could not take her to his prom, because his parents wanted him to take someone else. Turns out it was the tall, skinny, fair-skinned girl who was voted prom queen.

In college, the pretty boy she was dating brought his new girl to their graduation group dinner, boldly announcing that they were engaged. It was a slap in the face since he had gone out with Lisa a few times and they talked regularly. He had not said a word about having a girlfriend much less a fiancé.

The last straw happened after college. Lisa dated a few "regular looking" guys in the first few years after graduation, then met and soon married the very handsome Cameron Price. They moved from Houston to Los Angeles so he could pursue a modeling and acting career while she held down a nine-to-five to have a consistent flow of money for their living expenses.

He had gotten good jobs and did well financially for almost twenty years. When he aged out of modeling and the acting jobs dried up, his ego could not take it. He never had a "Plan B." In his mind, his life was rapidly declining. He sold drugs then started taking them. His death by drug overdose closed that chapter of her life and her interest in handsome men.

From that time until this day twenty-five years later, Lisa dated men who were nice enough looking and she was attracted to them, but they would not be considered especially handsome, and none gave her the vapors. They were fun and safe. Problem solved until Roman set his sights on her.

She had a feeling Roman would be back. They always come back when they are rejected, and it is always up to the woman to keep saying no. Lisa was not sure how many "no's" she had in her.

She had been dating Ben, a fellow church member, for a few weeks. He was a nice looking, smart, fun guy, but he did not give her the vapors.

Lisa dozed off at about four in the morning, wondering how she would navigate the times she would see Roman with his family. Would he stop staring at her? Could she look at him without sweat on her face and hands giving her thoughts away?

When her best friend from high school called at nine that morning, Lisa decided to confide in her since she was the one person who knew her history with extremely handsome men.

"Phyllis, I might be in trouble. Again." Lisa said out loud what she had been thinking.

"What kind of trouble? You're too old to be pregnant so what else could it be that's making you sound so scared?" Phyllis laughed. She was good at lightening the mood with the always-serious Lisa.

"How much time do you have? I need to purge. Maybe then I can think clearly."

"I've got all morning. My hair appointment is at one. Let me get my coffee and get comfortable."

Lisa got some water and sat on the sofa, taking a few deep breaths while she waited.

"Okay. Start at the beginning. I'll try not to interrupt." Phyllis liked to get the details right.

"So, remember I told you that I met this really nice older lady in my building a few months ago, the one who reminded me of my mom? Her name is Ruth Thompson. She is in her 90's and still a vibrant woman. You can tell she was a beauty in her day. And she still has all her faculties. I love sitting with her and listening to her stories about her husband, who is deceased, and their life together.

"She says I am the daughter she never had so we talk like mother and daughter about all kinds of things. Plus, I help her with her hair and getting new bath products. We even went to a spa for Valentine's Day for mani/pedis. She loved it. She said most of her female friends were gone so she didn't have anyone to do the girly stuff with and she was missing that until I started coming around.

"Anyway, Ms. Ruth has two sons. Two very, very handsome sons."

Phyllis groaned. She knew where this was going but she didn't say anything.

Chapter Seven

"I heard that groan. You already know where this is heading. The youngest son is Quincy, a semi-retired chef, smart and adorable. Tall, bald, muscular, dark chocolate, and super hilarious. He is like another brother to me. He lives with Ms. Ruth and takes great care of her.

"He and I have become very friendly. I even share my recipe files with him. He cooks all the time, so I have a standing invite to dinner on Thursdays when the whole family gathers to spend time with Ms. Ruth, as well as Sundays when it's just him and her. I always bring dessert since that is my favorite thing to make. No problems with him.

"Ms. Ruth has two very handsome grandsons: Eli and Danny. They are in their 20's and in graduate school. Eli looks just like his dad, Roman, Ms. Ruth's oldest son.

"Danny must look like his mother because of his fair skin and brown hair. Both are muscular and their dad is too. They say it's from working out in their home gym and all three playing basketball together.

"Ms. Ruth raised them, and they adore their "Granny" or "G" when they want to tease her. They cater to her every need. One of them will hang out with her when Quincy goes out or takes a catering job or a shift at the restaurant he used to own. She is so spoiled, but they say she spoiled them, so they are just giving her all the love that she deserves.

"Both of Ms. Ruth's grandsons write poetry, so I have attended a couple of poetry nights at Sugar's and watched them perform."

Phyllis had to comment, "So what's the problem? Oh, wait, the other son. What about him?"

"He is definitely the problem. Roman. I just met him in person, but I had seen all of his pictures from birth through college, marriage, work photos where he has won awards. Ms. Ruth loves pictures of her family and they are all on display on the wall as you walk into their apartment.

"Anyway, Roman is six feet tall, dark chocolate with wavy salt and pepper hair, a nice body that's solid, beautiful dark almond eyes, and a full, heart-shaped mouth that gives me lusty fantasies every time I look at him. He travels a lot for work, so he seems to come by when I'm at work, or out and about, or already in for the night.

"The day finally came for us to meet. I was headed to Ms. Ruth's for dinner with a pan of hot peach cobbler in my hands when the elevator door opened and there he was. In the flesh. Looking so handsome in one of those African outfits, you know, long shirt, almost to the knees, slender straight-legged pants, loafers. He smelled, oh my God, so good. I stepped back, startled, trying not to drop the pan. I could feel sweat forming on my face and hands. I couldn't speak so I just stared.

"He heard the elevator door open as he was about to walk by and was startled too. When he looked in and saw me, he stopped dead in his tracks, staring at me. As the door started to close, he put his hand in to stop it. Neither of us said a word until his sons bumped into him and saw why he stopped. The boys called my name and Danny took the dish out of my hands, making a beeline for the apartment so they could eat dinner and get to dessert. Roman and I still did not move and continued to look at each other for a few more seconds. It was awkward.

"I managed to avoid him most of the evening, sitting by Ms. Ruth. He stared at me the whole time, smiling like he knows something that no one else knows and it's amusing to him. I could not even look him in the face."

"Ahhh. Now we get to the good part." Phyllis was laughing.

"Yesterday he helped bring my groceries up and told me he wants us to date. I said no and gave him a bunch of reasons, but I know men. He will be back with some reasons of his own on why we should date. It's going to be hard to resist him. Help me, Phyllis. What can I do to keep saying no?"

Phyllis pushed back at Lisa. "Why say no? Have some fun with him. Get to know him. You might find that this is finally the one handsome man who will not break your heart. Give it a chance. The safe Mr. Ben hasn't been ringing your bell so let Roman have a shot.

"My guess is he will be nice since his whole family already knows you and likes you. He's not going to do anything to embarrass you or break your heart and make his family get on his case. Live a little. Stop letting the long-gone past control you."

Lisa was quiet for a minute and Phyllis waited patiently, listening to Lisa breathe. Phyllis finally spoke again.

"Stop over thinking this, Lisa. I would love a man who would get me hot and sweaty whenever I saw him. That would make for lots of fun and some good steamy sex. Why not? We are aging so how many more opportunities like this do you think we have?"

"I don't know Phyll. I love too hard. I can't risk it. My heartbreak with Cameron was enough for this lifetime. Thanks for listening though. I feel better about my decision."

They hung up, still on opposite sides, but Lisa was happy to be able to talk out loud about it. Now to prepare for Roman's next move. She knew it was coming.

Chapter Eight

Lisa did not have to wait long. She lived on the second floor in the end unit and her balcony faced the back of the building. All visitors and tenants had to use the long driveway from the street, pass her side of the building, the pool and lounge area, to get to the front of the building and parking.

She had tossed and turned in bed that night, unable to sleep so she went out on her balcony around midnight, dressed in a white print caftan, to enjoy the balmy weather and think about Roman's next possible move. She reminded herself that the man she was dating from church, Ben, was good enough.

An SUV slowly crept up the driveway. It stopped while still in her line of sight. Roman knew where her apartment was and could see that Lisa was on the balcony. He got out and stood facing her with his hands folded on top of the car. They stared at each other for a long moment before he spoke.

"I'm coming up. We need to talk." He didn't wait for her to respond before driving off to park. Her heart was racing as she went back into her apartment, checked her appearance, and waited until he tapped softly on her door.

When she opened the door, she noted how muscular and sexy he looked in his jeans, tee shirt, and loafers. She looked directly at him with a curious expression on her face, stepped back to let him in, then turned to make her way to the sofa. He stepped inside and locked the door.

They sat the same way they did the night before, with him facing her, their knees touching, and him holding her hands. She was stiff. He smiled, hoping to relax her.

"Something special happened between us that day at the elevator and we both know it. The more I have been around you, the more I want to be with you. Yes, I heard you yesterday. I have thought about what you said and want my chance to respond." He paused as she sat back on the sofa, pulled her hands away, crossed her arms, and said "Okaaay," curious about what he had to say.

"This whole pretty boy thing? Not me. How I look has to do with Ruth and Charles Thompson. And they taught me and Q not to get caught up in our looks because they could be taken away in one fight which I got into a lot of growing up. I appreciate how I look. I get a lot of attention because of it.

"My focus, however, has always been on my family, my work, and being healthy so I could raise my sons. I am a single father. Have been since Eli was just a few months old and now he is twenty-three. He and Danny depend on me. Neither of their mothers are in their lives. That is a story for another night. A date night." He paused as he said date night, and gave her a pointed look with his eyebrows raised. Lisa shook her head, smiling at his persistence.

"Anyway, I must admit though that I am happy that you like how I look. I want to be attractive to you just as you are to me. I think you are a very beautiful woman, which is part of the reason I stare at you so much when I see you.

"Now, to the vapors. That was a new one for me. Frankly, I love it! I like that I get you all hot and bothered just by being in my presence. It matches my excitement and makes my job a whole lot easier when it's time to move this relationship to the next level." He was smiling as he spoke.

Lisa spoke with her facial expressions, frowning at his presumptuousness, and turning her head away as she rolled her eyes.

"Yes, we are headed to another level. Together. Just hear me out."

Lisa looked at him again with eyebrows raised, curious about how he planned to get them to move forward together.

"I don't get the vapors the way you described, but like many men, I get giddy feelings and some anxiety when approaching a woman I'm interested in. I will tell you what I do get with you.

"When you say my name…my, my, my. You say it so softly, it sounds like you are stroking my ears, commanding, moaning, and pleading with me all at the same time to do something for you. To come to you. To help you.

"I get so turned on I could give you everything I have—money, house, cars, you can even have my children, just to hear you say my name again and let me do *whatever it is* that you need."

Lisa looked surprised, then they both started laughing.

Roman continued with a serious look on his face. "Men have their weaknesses too. Now you know mine. You are definitely my weakness. Truthfully? I like the way it feels." A slow smile spread across his face.

Lisa was smiling too, waiting for him to continue.

"Let me finish so that I don't keep you up all night and maybe I can get some sleep too.

"I don't have a 'type.' I mostly date women who approach me because I don't like or have time for the games. Maybe the tall thin ones are more assertive and not afraid to declare their interest so that's why I've dated more of them.

"I know you heard that I date a lot, and truthfully, for a while, in the last year or so, I was making up for lost time when my sons were growing up. I have been casually dating a couple of women off and on. More off than on really. My recent travel schedule has not been relationship friendly.

"In fact, I haven't been on dates or anything else with anyone in the last couple of months. I've been working on a new product launch which takes me out of town a lot to our manufacturing plants. That's why I'm just now meeting you.

"I want to date you. You act like you don't see me much less want to be bothered with me. Except the vapors give you away." He winked at her.

Chapter Nine

"Let me ask you about Mr. Genesis." Roman had learned some details about Lisa's man friend and date nights from Quincy.

"Yes, Quincy told me about you dating so I would hurry up and talk to you before you end up married to this other man."

Lisa looked surprised, then responded, "That's not his name. That's the car he drives. His name is..."

Roman cut her off. "I don't care what his name is. Are you sleeping with him?"

Lisa frowned. "That's none of your business."

"Well, I heard that he always drops you off at an appropriate hour after your dates, he never spends the night, and you never do the walk of shame, so I take that as a no. Good." Lisa rolled her eyes.

"Are you in an exclusive relationship with him?"

"No."

"So that means you are free to date me. Okay!" He nodded while smiling.

"One last issue you raised: I have direct access to your apartment. That is true. However, I would never come here uninvited – except tonight to plead my case – unless you were sick or in trouble and needed me. Promise. Scouts Honor.

"Did I leave anything out?"

Lisa shook her head no. She was impressed with his comments but still not convinced to date him.

"Okay then. I'm going to leave you to get some rest. Just to be clear, this is your official notice. I'm coming for you, Woman. I want you. You want me too. You are letting your history dictate today. That's not acceptable. And to use a term you might like from the olden days, I'm going to court you, show you who I am and how I can care for you with the hope that you will let me into your life, your heart, your bed, and all the other things that go with having a relationship.

"We have a lot to do together in and out of town—dates, shopping, traveling. I need those things to start happening sooner rather than later. Get ready. Now walk me to the door."

He helped her up from the sofa, leading the way, and just as he was about to reach the door, he turned around and swept her up in his arms.

"Kiss me good night, Woman," he whispered as he kissed her ear, then her nose. When he got to her mouth, she was about to protest when he placed his mouth over hers. They paused, both liking the feel of their lips pressing together.

He liked kissing and had a technique he had practiced over the years. He never rushed, always taking his time, savoring the mouth and tongue like a blind man reading braille.

She did not pull away. Instead, her arms went around his waist and she leaned into him. He cradled her head in the bend of his arm and put the other arm around her waist, pulling her to him as he leaned back on the door. Their tongues did a slow dance, getting to know one another. It felt like home to them both and they moaned at the same time, him because her lips were so soft and she tasted sweet; her because she finally got to taste the man she had been dreaming about since the night at the elevator and it was *good,* better than she had imagined.

Roman's kissing technique was perfection. He did not try to choke her by putting his tongue down her throat, or go too fast, or give wet sloppy kisses. His lips were soft, just moist enough, he took his time, and the soft pressure of his lips on hers made her want more.

He began to rub his lips back and forth across her lips to start disconnecting but somehow his tongue kept slipping back in her mouth. Finally, he kissed her cheek and whispered in her ear, "I am definitely coming for you, Woman. I want you. I want more of this. A lot more."

They parted slowly and he opened the door, looking back at her. She was shaking her head no, rubbing her face, and whispering, "God help me."

He heard her and responded quietly, "He will. God's going to help me be good to you. I just need you to let me."

She closed the door and leaned on it, licking her lips and savoring his taste in her mouth.

He went through the door across the hall so he could walk down the steps and out to his car to help work out the heat in his body that had built up with the kissing.

Neither one of them slept much that night. Roman was creating a plan and plotting on how to put it in place. Lisa was praying for strength not to give in to his pressure.

Chapter Ten

Roman believed that Lisa would not be interested in flowers or cards or a lot of calls. That was too obvious for now and she would probably be annoyed instead of flattered.

His plan was simple: the soft and subtle approach--soften her up when he spent time around her and the family, let her get to know him, partner with her when they played games, do the little things that showed he was attentive to her and learning about her.

On the flip side, he wanted her to miss him so her reaction to his long work hours or trips out of town for work would help gauge whether his plan was working. He hoped that within thirty days, she would be ready to let him break through that wall she was using to avoid him.

The next Thursday, Roman put his plan into action. He was already at his Mom's place when Lisa came down with lemon pound cake and frozen vanilla yogurt for dessert.

He watched how much food she put on her plate and whether she used salt and pepper or condiments so he would know how to fix her plate the next time. She liked a bottle of chilled water after dinner, so she put it in the freezer when she was getting ready to eat. Just as she finished, she would get her water and drink it. Then she waited to have dessert while everyone else ate theirs right away. Except Roman.

He sat next to her at dinner but mostly talked to Quincy about work and the week ahead while she talked to Ms. Ruth, Danny, and Eli.

When Lisa got dessert, Roman got his too so he could talk to her.

"What's on your agenda for the week?" Roman asked.

"Not much. Work, errands, the usual."

"Plans for the weekend?" Roman wanted to ask about Mr. Genesis but not directly so he would not seem jealous.

"Yes." Lisa was not forthcoming with any other information. She had a standing date with Ben on Fridays, but this weekend he was going out of town to see his daughters. Her plan was to meet up with friends for happy hour but Roman did not need to know any of that.

After dinner, Roman sat by the patio door and had a good view of Lisa as she moved around in the kitchen, helping Quincy clean up. Occasionally she would catch him looking at her with an amused smile on his face. He was also rubbing his mustache and beard, a sign that Danny had said meant that Roman was in deep thought.

At the end of the evening, he watched her walk out the door and wished her well until next time. She was disappointed that he had not offered to walk her to her apartment.

Friday night was her night out with the girls. Roman watched her leave in her own car, believing she was meeting Mr. Genesis somewhere. When she came back at midnight, he was waiting for her on his Mom's patio.

"Did you give him his two-week notice?" Roman startled her when he spoke. There were no lights coming from the apartment so she did not see him until he stepped to the edge of the patio.

"Why are you still here? Is Ms. Ruth okay?"

"Yes, she's fine. Asleep. You didn't answer my question."

"Why would I do that? I told you, he's a nice guy and I enjoy his company."

"Nothing wrong with that. I'm looking forward to my time with you. I hope he doesn't mind sharing." Roman was not usually the jealous type, mostly because he was not that invested in most of the women he had dated after Eli was born. With Lisa, he could feel those emotions bubbling up.

Roman was missing in action the next week so it was two weeks before she saw him again. On Thursday, there was a repeat of Roman watching Lisa during dinner and dessert – sweet potato pie this time.

They watched Ms. Ruth's favorite game shows: Wheel of Fortune, Jeopardy, and Family Feud. The family kept score on who got the most answers right and when Lisa and Roman tied, he high-fived her and held her hand an extra moment. She did not pull away, instead she waited for him to let her hand go.

Sunday Lisa went to the Thompson apartment for dinner with Ms. Ruth and Quincy, but Roman walked in about twenty minutes after she did. Quincy must have let him know she was there.

He made his first bold move. He fixed her plate and served it to her as if he was a waiter, with a towel draped over his arm. She was surprised and laughed as he made a big production, bowing at the waist, introducing himself as "Ro-mahn," her waiter, and calling her Beautiful Woman.

"This is good Ro-mahn. Just like I like it. How did you know?" Lisa did not realize how closely he had been watching her.

He smiled when she called his name, then responded softly, "I am studying you. I want to know everything about you so I can do things for you."

Lisa could only shake her head and blush.

Just as she finished eating and was ready for her water, it appeared in his hand. He presented it to her like it was a bottle of fine vintage wine, asking, "Is it to your liking, Beautiful Woman?"

She joined in the game, giving him a snooty, "It will do Ro-mahn. Thank you." She loved his playfulness and sense of humor. She also knew how he felt when she called his name, so she did it as often as she dared without looking obvious.

Dessert was apple cobbler. He heated up a large scoop and had ice cream in a bowl on the side with two spoons on a small tray. They sat on the sofa together and she took a scoop of the cobbler. He fed her ice cream with his spoon. Why not, Lisa reasoned to herself. They had already kissed. She just hoped that no one noticed that Roman was feeding her.

No such luck. Ms. Ruth and Quincy smiled at each other, knowing that Roman was pulling out all of the stops. Eli and Danny had stopped by for dessert and high fived each other quietly in the kitchen, hoping that Lisa would marry into their family and they would finally have a Mom.

Chapter Eleven

Roman went out of town the next week and Lisa missed him. When she was with the family on Thursday, she kept looking at the door, expecting, or at least hoping, that he would walk in.

Ms. Ruth noticed and whispered to her, "Are you okay baby?"

"Yes, fine. Why do you ask?"

"I see you looking at the door. He's not coming back until Saturday. Call him. I'm sure he would love to hear from you."

Lisa became flustered when she realized she was so obvious.

"I'm good. Thanks."

Roman was back at his Mom's on Sunday. Lisa got there first and was talking to Ms. Ruth when he came in. When she looked up and into his eyes, he was looking at her and winked. She looked down and gave an involuntary moan and whispered, "Lord I want that man in my body *and* my soul."

Ms. Ruth heard Lisa and was surprised, looked at her, then broke out into a hard loud laugh. Everyone turned to see what made Ms. Ruth react so heartily.

Lisa looked at her then realized what she had done. She was embarrassed and turned red, whispering as she rose hurriedly from the sofa, "I'd better go. I did not mean to say that out loud."

Before she could get to the door, Ms. Ruth stopped laughing long enough to tell her sons, "Do not let her out of this house."

Roman was happy to step in front of her, curious as to why she was in such a hurry all of a sudden, and what had led his Mother to demand that Lisa stay.

Lisa walked back over to sit with Ms. Ruth and apologized. "I am truly sorry. That was so inappropriate. I did not mean to say that out loud."

"I bet you didn't." Ms. Ruth replied, still laughing. Then she whispered, "It's okay. I felt like that about his dad the first day I laid eyes on him and most days after. You have been touched by a Thompson. He likes you too. I don't know why you won't go out with him. He's a good guy. He likes taking care of us. He would take good care of you too."

"Sure, for a while." Lisa shared her concern. "I'm not good with such handsome men and I would not know what to do if my feelings got hurt. It would be hard to be around you and the rest of the family."

"What makes you think your feelings would be hurt? He needs a good woman, a good relationship, and you're a good woman. Sounds like a love match to me." Ms. Ruth stopped laughing and gave Lisa a serious look. "Don't be afraid dear. Give him a chance. He might surprise you."

Lisa whispered, "Ms. Ruth, I can't with you. You're supposed to be looking out for me, your daughter. Sounds like you are playing matchmaker for your son."

"I am looking out for you. Mother knows best." Ms. Ruth winked at Lisa, then they turned to watch the first show of the evening.

Roman and Quincy looked at each other and shrugged, still not sure of what had just transpired to make their Mom laugh like she had not laughed in a long time.

Quincy finally asked, "What was so funny?"

Ms. Ruth smiled at Lisa and said, "Nothing for you. It's between me and Lisa. Is dinner ready?"

Lisa was quiet, thinking of what Ms. Ruth said. Would it be a love match or just lust, and once fulfilled, would it fizzle out? She asked to be excused before dinner was served. Ms. Ruth gave her a hug and this time let her leave.

Roman wanted to walk Lisa to her place and ask what was wrong, but when he looked at his Mom with a questioning look, she shook her head, "No." She thought Lisa needed to have time to think about what she wanted to do without Roman putting pressure on her.

Roman was missing in action again all of the next week. Not out of town but busy at the office so he was working long hours.

Meanwhile, Ben noticed Lisa was quiet on their next Friday night date and realized she had been quiet the past couple of weeks. He decided to inquire about the change in her.

"Are you okay? You seem different these last few weeks. Quiet. Sad even sometimes. Are you feeling okay? Is it something I said?"

Lisa lied. "Everything's good. Sorry to worry you." She gave a phony smile then turned her complete attention to him. Roman had filled her head and was cracking open her heart and she was terrified. Ben did not need to know that even though they were friends and she felt she could confide in him.

When Sunday came, Lisa could hardly sit still in church. She was eager to get home and see if Roman was there. He was waiting on the patio when she drove up.

Chapter Twelve

It was a hot, sunny, end-of June Sunday so Lisa was wearing her sunglasses when she got out of the car. She did not want him to see her eyeing him from head to toe in his shorts, tight pullover Polo shirt, and tennis shoes. His legs were long with muscles from his hip to his ankles. So sexy, Lisa imagined her legs rubbing his, igniting a serious sexual fire.

Roman walked over to her car so he could speak with her in private before she came down to be with the family.

"Hey, Woman." Roman had heard that Lisa was quiet all week so he was looking in her face to see if he could figure out what was going on.

"Hi." Lisa was tense, waiting to see what else he would say.

"How was your week?"

"It was good. Quiet. How was yours?"

"The usual crazy busy for a new project. Did you give Mr. Genesis his notice yet?"

"No."

"Well, are you ready for us to have our first date?"

"No thanks."

Roman had a feeling she was starting to weaken but she was still not quite ready for him yet. He wanted to get to her apartment again and kiss her to remind her of what they could have together. Truthfully, he wanted another kiss just because they were so good.

"How about this," he offered as they walked to the door of the building. "My sons are reading at Sugar's on Thursday. Let's start with something light and fun. We can go together. I'm sure they will want their personal cheerleader there." He gave her a pointed look, acknowledging that she was their favorite cheerleader.

Lisa hesitated before responding. She had planned to go but did not want that to be a "date night" for them. She countered, "How about I meet you there? I have a class so I can't get there until late. It gets crowded fast so save me a seat."

Roman's ears perked up. He did not know about her being in school.

Once they were inside her apartment he asked, "What kind of class are you taking? Is this new? You are always at Moms at 6:30 when dinner is served, why is this week different?"

"I'm not taking a class, I'm teaching one. Filling in for someone who is going on vacation."

"What do you teach? In fact, what do you do?" He was eager to start filling in some of the gaps in her life that he knew nothing about. Quincy had given him highlights. He now wanted details.

"Throughout my work life I've been in the health industry, specifically as executive director of a few different community healthcare centers. I am semi-retired and now work as a certified diabetes care manager.

"I teach classes at one of the centers and work with individuals with diabetes while other people do the heavy lifting at the top. My classes are usually in the daytime two or three days a week so I can have evenings free. Except this week as I fill-in for the other instructor."

"Ahhh," Roman thought as he spoke. "That's right, you are the one who finally convinced Q to lighten up on the salt and rice and pastas that he cooks. And your desserts are delicious. Can't tell that they are not made the old-fashioned way with tons of sugar and butter. We are all eating healthier. Thank you.

"So back to Thursday. I'll be there with a seat for you. What time will you be there?"

"About eight. I'll text you when I arrive."

"Okay. Are you ready to head downstairs for Thompson family night? Where is dessert?" He was looking around the kitchen and in the oven.

"It's in the fridge. You can carry it while I lock up." Lisa was happy to have him in her apartment. She was weakening but still didn't want to give in. She was about to open the refrigerator door when he touched her elbow and pulled her in to lean on his body as he stood at the counter.

"I missed you, Woman. I missed hearing your voice," he whispered as he licked his lips, preparing to kiss her.

Lisa smiled to herself, happy to hear that he had missed her. She wondered why he had not called, then she realized he was playing with her, testing to see if she missed him.

This kiss started out like the first one – soft lips pressing together, and the tongue dance was slow, firm, and possessive. Then he leaned in and his tongue was more aggressive. He rubbed her back with both hands and started a trail of kisses from her lips to her ear.

"Did you miss me too? Did you think of me? Of us kissing like this?"

Before she could respond, he slid his tongue in her mouth again. Her nipples stood at attention, pushing forward to rest on his firm chest. She wrapped her arms around him to steady herself when she felt her legs weakening. She also realized how nice his body felt and how good he smelled. It was going to be a long night.

Chapter Thirteen

A call from Quincy to hurry, dinner was ready, forced them to stop. They both moaned and their foreheads touched as he released her. Looking into her eyes he promised, "We are not done, Woman. I'm going to need a kiss goodnight."

Lisa's excitement and anticipation showed in her eyes.

Roman busied himself with getting dessert from the fridge. She had learned everyone's favorite dessert and made it for each of them over the last couple of months: Ms. Ruth loved German chocolate cake, Quincy's favorite was sweet potato pie, and Eli and Danny ate any cobbler as long as there was lots of crust and juice. Homemade cookies were a never fail dessert that everyone liked.

Tonight it was an old-fashioned lemon icebox pie, Roman's favorite Lisa had learned, and her way of saying "Welcome Home." He knew as soon as he saw it that it was a gift to him. It was the sign he needed to believe his plan was working. She missed him.

Roman was quiet all through dinner and dessert, rubbing his beard until his Mom finally looked at him and asked if he was all right.

"Yes, I'm fine," he said. "Actually though, Lisa and I need to talk so we have to say an early goodnight."

They all looked at Lisa who had been relaxed and having fun. Once Roman spoke, she frowned and looked at Roman, wondering what they needed to talk about.

They walked back to Lisa's apartment in silence while holding hands. She couldn't figure out what had happened after their kissing session to warrant such an abrupt end to the Sunday evening. In her mind, a kiss goodnight did not warrant an early departure from family time.

When they got inside the apartment, Roman asked her to leave the lights off except for one lamp, and then walked over to the sofa to sit. He motioned for her to come sit with him. She waited for him to talk. He leaned back and pulled her into his arms then quietly shared with her why he wanted to leave the family early.

"The project I'm working on is very important to the company so there are a lot of meetings and many decisions to be made that fall on my shoulder to orchestrate. The next couple of days are going to be especially intense.

"You are so calm and peaceful, I just wanted to have some time to be alone with you and draw strength from you. You make me feel centered and grounded so I can go back into the world and get things done.

"It is selfish, and please tell me if you have a problem with this. I can tell that being around you more will level out the intense times in my life." He paused and looked in her eyes before he spoke again.

"Are you okay with this? I don't want to impose."

"It's fine Roman. Would you like something to drink? Some music? To talk? Or just be quiet? Not sure what you want me to do."

"Nothing to drink. Music is good. Something soft like smooth jazz or piano music. We can talk or be quiet. You decide. I just want to be close to you for a little while."

Lisa knew intuitively that he needed quiet so she raised up to ask Alexa to play soft piano music at a low volume then turned back toward Roman to lay in his arms . It felt good to her too. Very relaxing. She knew she could easily get used to this as a special time for them together. Her life was not intense like his, but she liked being in his arms and being needed by him.

After about an hour, Roman felt much better and got ready to leave. When he got to the door, he thanked her for being so supportive, then stepped to Lisa whose back was against the wall. He placed her head at the angle he wanted, and then placed his lips on hers. His arms wrapped around her and he slowly rubbed her body from her neck to her butt. For the next twenty minutes he slowly kissed and rubbed her like he was possessed—lips, cheeks, eyes, nose, forehead, squeezing and pressing her body to his while whispering in her ear how much he needed her in his life, needed to talk to her and kiss her every day.

Lisa felt the urgency in his hands and mouth and knew the exact moment she slipped under his spell. Her arms went around his waist and she began to rub his back and moan in his mouth.

She wanted him too, but fear still stood in her way.

Chapter Fourteen

The day finally came to go to Sugar's for poetry night. It was a full day for Lisa, and she was excited knowing she was going to meet up with Roman. It was a test run for her to see if she really wanted to risk her emotions again.

She rushed home to change into a sexy top, tight jeans, and heels that made her legs look long. She arrived at Sugar's promptly at eight and went inside. The place was crowded as usual so it took her a minute to spot Roman, Eli, and Danny at the table in the center of the room. It was a square table for four, and all the seats were filled. A woman was sitting in the fourth chair, and she looked like she had been there a minute—purse hanging off the chair, jacket open on the back of the chair, and she looked comfortable.

When Roman left the table to walk to the window, the woman picked up Roman's beer and took a sip, making sure to put it back in the exact spot. Lisa's heart dropped.

She did not know who the woman was and hesitated to intrude. Did Roman forget that she was coming tonight? Did he think that she was not coming so he didn't save her a seat? Was he playing her with another woman on their first night out? Lisa decided to grab the last seat at the bar and watch the Thompson men, especially Roman, for a few minutes.

Roman kept looking around the room for Lisa, checking his phone, and going to the window to see if he could see her car. He was getting anxious, especially since his ex-wife, Gloria, had shown up unexpectedly, and plopped down in the seat he was saving for Lisa, refusing to get up until the "mystery woman" came.

Roman never said who was coming, only that he was saving the seat, and kept repeating that she had to leave. Gloria knew it had to be a woman, so she wanted to see who it was and try to interfere with whatever Roman had going on with her.

Gloria had a long-standing feud with Roman who never forgave her for leaving him and Eli when Eli was not even a year old. She tried to come back to them when Eli was three, then five, and again when he was twelve, but each time Roman refused to take her back.

Gloria and Eli had developed a cordial relationship when he was twelve, talking when she initiated the calls and having lunch every month or two when his school and sports schedule allowed. She had apologized to him for leaving and wanted to try to have a relationship, but she thought he never seemed to warm up to her.

Truth was that Eli was indifferent to her. She had never been around for him to get to know and miss her as a mother. His Granny had given him all of the mothering he needed. He tolerated Gloria because his dad said she was his mother so he should be open to forming a relationship.

Gloria had finally accepted motherhood when Eli was three and was determined to bond with him so she had spent years trying to be in his life. He had mentioned their schedule at Sugar's weeks before, but had no idea she would show up. She never had before.

Eli knew that Ms. Lisa was coming and had a bad feeling about how the night would go for his dad. When Gloria showed up, Roman looked at Eli with a frown. Eli frowned too and shrugged, mouthing, "I'm sorry. I didn't know."

Lisa sent a text to Roman. "I came as promised, but I see there is no seat at the table for me. Enjoy the show." She watched Roman read the text and jump up from his seat.

He walked to the front of the room, next to the stage, and slowly crisscrossed the floor, row by row, until he got to the back of the room and entry door, hoping to see her. He even went outside to search the small parking lot.

He came back inside, determined to find her. He decided to take a second look at the bar and there she was. The end seat where she sat was in a dark area, so he had missed her during his first look.

Chapter Fifteen

Lisa was chatting with the man sitting next to her, Johnny Mack, and waiting for her Moscato when Roman stood behind her and planted his hands on the bar ledge on each side of her, his arms blocking her in. She looked down at his hands but did not turn around, gathering her thoughts on how to handle this moment.

Roman whispered in her right ear. "I'm glad you didn't leave. We need to talk so I can explain about the seat. That woman is Eli's mother, my ex-wife, Gloria. She likes to start trouble in my life. I had no idea she was coming."

Lisa turned her head slightly toward his voice and looked at his arm, not in his face. "No need to talk. I am here for Danny and Eli. You should go back to your seat before they think you are not coming back. Enjoy the show."

You could feel the heat rising in Roman's body and not in a good sexy way. He was angry with Gloria for intruding and upset with himself for not grabbing another table or chair. He knew this was a major setback in his efforts to appeal to Lisa given her trust issues and decided to rectify the situation immediately. Just as he was about to ask Lisa to leave with him so they could talk, Gloria walked up and stood next to Roman.

"Oh, so this is your flavor of the month huh? Okay, she's cute."

Still facing forward, Lisa took a sip of her drink and waited. Roman responded to Gloria in a harsh tone that Lisa had never heard from him before.

"Get away from us Gloria. Do not go back to the table, and do not say another word. LEAVE NOW."

"Okay, I'll go. But first let me tell Ms. Thang something."

Lisa picked up her drink then turned to look at Gloria with a curious expression. She looked Gloria up and down then looked at Roman and back at Gloria, waiting to hear what she had to say.

"I'm Gloria, Roman's wife and Eli's mother."

"Ex-wife, from over twenty years ago." Roman was quick to point out. "I know what your game is, Gloria. You are a liar and troublemaker. You are angry that I don't want you, haven't since you left, so you always want to make trouble. GO AWAY."

"So why are you in my face?" Lisa interjected.

"Oh, I always like to meet his drive-bys. You should know he likes variety, so don't expect him to be around long term. Enjoy him while you can. He is a good man and will show you a real good time. Real good." When she said that, Gloria looked at Roman and licked her lips.

"But just know that sooner or later, he will lose interest and come back home." She patted her chest to indicate that she was home for Roman and looked at him. "And you always come back home, don't you baby?"

Gloria turned back to Lisa. "Just giving you a heads up."

Lisa fake smiled and shrugged as she dismissed her. "Okay, thanks. Well, you can leave now. I'm sure he will call you when it's your turn again."

Gloria was surprised at Lisa's comeback. The other women she had seen Roman with would be upset and leave in a huff when Gloria spoke to them. This one was going to be a challenge, a thorn in Gloria's plan to get Roman back, yes, even after all these years.

Roman's head snapped around to look at Lisa. He hoped her comments were meant to sting with Gloria but also let him know that she wasn't as upset as he thought.

Lisa took another look at Roman, then turned back around on the bar stool to take another sip of her drink. What she needed was some Jack Daniels and coke, but the Moscato would just have to do. She only had one drink when she was driving.

Gloria was lying, but she just wanted to plant a seed of doubt in this woman's mind that Roman would be a good man for her. If Gloria couldn't have Roman, she did not want anyone else to enjoy him either. He was a good man and she had ruined a great relationship. The price she paid in losing him and her son was regrettable but did not stop her from wreaking havoc when she could. Instead of taking full responsibility and living her life without them or what she could have with Eli, she kept inserting herself wherever she could and would do so until Eli stopped answering her calls.

Roman gave Gloria one last warning. "Either you leave now, or I will make sure Eli knows the truth about you and all that you have done." She caved.

"Okay, okay. Tell Eli I will call him tomorrow." With those words and one last look at Lisa, Gloria left. There was something about the way Roman had paced the floor waiting for her and was standing so close behind Lisa at the bar, that let Gloria know that Lisa was important to Roman. She did not want to think about what that could mean.

Roman put his hands back on the bar on either side of Lisa. He was momentarily at a loss for words. They needed to leave Sugar's and go to a quiet place so he could explain.

He whispered in her ear, "Let's get out of here. We really need to talk. Tonight. Please can we go now?"

Lisa did not have time to respond because just then, Danny and Eli were called to the stage. They were trying out a new poetry duet they had created plus they each had one poem to perform.

Lisa shared with Johnny Mack that these were the young men she came to hear. Roman moved from behind Lisa to stand at her side so they could both look at the boys as they performed. She did not want to look at Roman. There were no vapors this time. Just a growing recognition that there would likely never be a "Lisa and Roman."

Chapter Sixteen

As soon as their set was over, Eli and Danny came over to the bar. Eli could see his dad was rubbing his face and looking frustrated, no doubt from the encounter with Gloria. He apologized to Lisa.

"I'm sorry about the mishap at the table with your seat Ms. Lisa. We tried to get Gloria to leave but she refused. I had no idea she was coming because she never has before. Don't be mad at Pops please. I don't know if he has told you about her, but she is a piece of work. Likes to start trouble."

Lisa took note of the fact that he called his mother by her first name. She smiled at him and thanked him for his explanation. "It's all good Eli. I got to see you guys which was more important than her shenanigans. You were great by the way! The duet was genius! I'm going to head out now. I'll see you another time."

As Lisa slid off the bar stool, Roman wrapped his hand around her arm between her shoulder and elbow and threw his key fob to Eli. "Take my car when you leave here. Ms. Lisa and I are going to the house to talk and we will take her car." He didn't ask Lisa, just took control.

Roman guided Lisa out the door and she led him to her car. He put her in the passenger seat and got in on the driver's side. Neither said a word all the way to his house.

The house smelled like very soft masculine cologne when Lisa walked in. It was two levels, and all of the large first floor family room was decorated in oversized brown leather furniture with wood tables. Family pictures were everywhere, mostly his sons in their athletic gear, award ceremonies, graduation gowns, prom photos...all occasions were chronicled with a picture, similar to his Mom's house.

Roman brought her a bottle of water and asked her to sit on the sofa. He sat across from her in a recliner, leaning forward, still scowling as he replayed the events at Sugar's in his mind. Lisa took a sip of water and waited for him to speak.

"Thank you for coming here. I really want to talk tonight and not let what happened keep us from being together. I have a strong feeling that if you had gone home tonight without us talking that you would definitely shut down the possibilities of us. You still might, but I hope you will hear me out first."

The look on his face softened to the look he always gave her, a look that said, "I care about you and like us being together."

He took a deep breath and began sharing the story of his marriage in a matter-of-fact tone. There was no anger or bitterness.

"I married late in life, in my 40's, after building my career in production operations for a couple different auto parts manufacturing companies. Gloria was in her mid-30's, an only child from a nice family, and they spoiled her rotten.

"What I learned soon after we married was that she saw me as a cash machine who would pick up where her parents left off, buying her whatever she wanted. When I realized it and reigned in her credit card spending, she told me we were pregnant.

"I was thrilled and ready to be a father. I became much more conservative in spending to be sure we had what we needed for the baby long term, you know, like a college fund and money for good schools and to take him or her on nice vacations.

"Gloria had the baby and about eight months later said she did not want to be a mother. I came home one day and she was gone. Left Eli with the neighbor and a note on our kitchen table saying she couldn't take me or the baby anymore."

Roman paused, checking Lisa's face to see if she was reacting to what he was saying. Her face was blank but watchful.

"Can I get you anything? More water? Something to eat? I cooked today and there is plenty left over." Lisa shook her head no. He continued.

"I thought it was what is now known as postpartum depression and she would get some help and come back after a month or two. It took over two years for her to show her face again. By then I was long over her. I had bought a house and Eli and I were in a routine. My dad had died so mom moved in with us to take care of Eli while I worked. On the weekends, I spent all of my time with him. It has been like that ever since. I wanted him to know that I would never leave him like his mother had done.

"Gloria came back a couple more times using Eli as the excuse and trying to seduce me into taking her back. I never slept with her. In fact, the last time I did was before she had the baby. After that, she was always healing from the delivery or just not in the mood, then gone.

"She has a knack for showing up in unexpected places and pretends that we are still married or that I want her back. I took a restraining order out on her once because she tried to take Eli from school a couple of times without permission.

"She has come up to my job screaming and crying that I was keeping her away from her only child. Thankfully, management understood, but I had to take drastic measures to keep her away from us. She has broken out the windows of my cars, and since social media, has posted pictures of me and warning women that I am mean and keeping her from her child.

"After she put on one of her most recent performances, I threatened to put another restraining order on her. She doesn't seem to care unless I threaten to have her put in jail. She thinks I am playing but I'm not. When I let her know that I will tell Eli the truth about her, it stops her from going too far."

Lisa asked for the bathroom. She needed a moment to process what he was saying. She wondered what Roman might have done to provoke Gloria to such drastic actions, not able to imagine leaving her child or being so bitter that she acted out the way he described. On the other hand, women were known to do crazy things when it came to their regrets with a man and efforts to get him back. Or destroy him.

Chapter Seventeen

When Lisa went back to the family room, the boys were walking in the front door. Eli and Danny were both quiet, trying to read the room before saying too much. Eli apologized again.

"Please don't be mad at our dad Ms. Lisa. He was trying not to cause a scene and mess things up for us for poetry night. Gloria was refusing to leave. Short of dumping her out of the chair onto her butt there wasn't much he could do." Danny was afraid Lisa would leave and not be interested in Roman anymore.

Lisa gave them a halfhearted smile, responding, "It's all good. No worries." Roman was watching her, hoping that she meant what she said.

The boys said goodnight and headed to bed. Lisa was ready to leave and asked Roman if he had said all that he wanted to say because she wanted to get home.

"It's late. Don't leave. Spend the night here with us. I'll fix breakfast tomorrow before you go home."

Lisa frowned and her voice level went up an octave. "Are you kidding me? I would never spend the night here. Your sons are upstairs."

Roman laughed. "And? They are grown men. Are you saying that if we are dating and sleeping together that you will not spend nights here with me? Or us?"

"That is correct. How could they respect me and I'm laying up with their dad in the house that you all share? If we are not married--No Sir. They can guess about what we do if you are not at home but I will not provide receipts."

"Okay, then marry me and that will take care of that."

"Roman. Stop playing. You know what I'm saying."

He paused before he continued, looking at her with a very serious expression. "I'm not playing."

His seriousness caught Lisa off guard. She did a double take, looking at him with raised eyebrows.

"Okay, yes, I get it," Roman continued. "We don't have to sleep in the bed. We can sleep right here, with all of our clothes on. I just don't want you to go yet. I need to tell you about Danny. See this is why we should be dating, so we could have these discussions over dinner or some other activity."

"You can tell me now and then I'll leave. Just make it quick."

Roman breathed a heavy sigh then continued. "First, you need to know that I've only been married once and that was to Gloria. Second, I do not have a baby mama.

"When Eli started kindergarten, he and Danny immediately became good friends. Danny never seemed to have enough to eat and was always hungry so Eli started sharing his lunch with him. After the first week, he would have Mom pack two lunches every day so Danny had his own.

"We found out Danny and his Mom, Roberta, were living with her elderly grandmother. Roberta never worked because she had sickle cell and was sick all the time, in and out of hospitals. The story was Roberta's mother died when she was young and it traumatized her. She ended up having Danny right after high school graduation. Her grandmother, who was a domestic, raised her. There was very little money left for food after the house note and utilities were paid, and Roberta got her medications, which is why Danny was always hungry.

"Roberta's grandmother died, and Roberta was in the hospital a lot. Danny's dad was not around. Roberta had no family to look after her. Danny would stay with us when she went to the hospital and on weekends and my Mom would buy him clothes so he would look nice and fit in like the other kids.

"When we found out how sick she was, we started looking after her too. She didn't want to move in with us so Mom would go over when the kids were in school and make sure she ate and bathed and took her medicine. Mom also washed their clothes and cleaned the house.

"One day, when the boys were in second grade, late in the school year, Danny's mother called Mom to say she was in the hospital and would not be able to take care of Danny anymore. She was dying. She asked if we could take Danny permanently. If not, he would be taken to Child Protective Services and into the foster care system.

"By then he was not just Eli's friend, he was family. I took Danny to the hospital to see her and say goodbye, then she and I talked. She signed over the house to me for Danny and I adopted him. There are tenants in the house and the rent goes toward taxes and upkeep. The rest goes into an account so he will have some money once he turns thirty."

"Why are you telling me all of this tonight?" Lisa asked.

"Because I need you to know these things so you will know who I am and that I am worthy of your time, Woman. I don't want you to leave here with only the experience with Gloria in your head.

"Besides, I need us to plan a real date where you get dressed up for me instead of Mr. Genesis, and I take you somewhere nice instead of us meeting up."

"Okay Mr. True Confession, what about the women in your life now? Who looks for you to visit on a regular basis whether you call it a relationship or not?"

"I told you I haven't dated anyone seriously in a while. First, I did not want to take time away from Eli and Danny, and I didn't want them to see me with different women all the time, so I mostly dated when I would go on business trips. Now that my sons are adults, I have started going out in town more but still no one is looking for me. I told you, my travel schedule has been brutal lately."

By this time, Lisa was exhausted and had yawned several times. She stood to leave. "I hear you Mr. Thompson. Right now though, I just need to go home and to bed. Goodnight."

Roman walked her to the door. Instead of kissing her mouth, he held her in his arms and kissed her forehead, then walked her to her car.

"I'm going to follow you home to be sure you get there okay."

Lisa was about to protest when Roman added, "It's late and you are tired. Think about what I have said on your way home so you will stay awake."

When they got to her building, she parked and walked over to his car to say goodnight again. She had thought of all that he said on the way home and was less anxious about the night.

"Thank you for sharing tonight even though it was not necessary."

"I'll call you tomorrow, Woman. Now go to bed. No balcony tonight." They both smiled.

Chapter Eighteen

For the next two weeks, Lisa spent Thursdays with the Thompson family as if nothing had changed. Only something had changed. Lisa knew she had been weakening until poetry night. After that, she re-confirmed in her mind that being with Roman would not be a good idea. She did not like drama, and Gloria would be drama whenever she came around. Lisa led a quiet calm life and did not want that to change.

She was relaxed around Roman and looked him in the eye when they spoke or played games together, but she was more cordial to him than friendly and open. No lingering handholding or long looks.

He could feel the difference in how she responded to him and knew he was back to square one in trying to get her to go out with him. He was often seen stroking his mustache and beard, in deep thought as he gazed at her.

He watched and waited for an opportunity to reconnect with her. It came on Sunday, July 13th.

Lisa sent a text to the group early that morning as she was leaving the building. She said that she would not attend Sunday dinner but would have some Crave cupcakes delivered. It was not the first time she had missed Sunday dinner, but before she had let them know what she was up to so they would not worry. Both Ms. Ruth and Quincy wondered if she was okay. Quincy asked in a text, but she never responded. Lisa had turned her phone off for the day.

Dinner was at five on Sundays, so Lisa got back home just before three, hoping to avoid seeing any of them on the patio. As she pulled into the parking lot, she saw Roman's car was there. Lisa prayed that he was already inside, visiting with his Mom and brother. He was inside, but he was watching the parking lot for her.

Lisa was taking too long to get out of the car so Roman knew something was wrong. He hurried over to the driver's side and noticed that Lisa's head was resting on the back of the seat, her eyes were closed, and she was fidgeting with her keys. She could feel his presence so she wiped her face, put her sunglasses on, turned the car off, and opened the door, stepping out.

Lisa spoke first. "Please Roman. Not today. I need to get to my apartment. I already sent the text that I was not coming to dinner so go on back to your Moms."

"Not until you tell me what is wrong." He stepped in front of her and took her sunglasses off. Her eyes were swollen and red.

"What is wrong? Are you hurt?" He rubbed her arms and felt her back.

Lisa shook her head no.

"Why have you been crying? Did Mr. Genesis say or do something to you today?"

Lisa shook her head no again.

"Were you in an accident?"

"No. Please just let me go to my apartment."

He walked alongside her.

"Then what is it? Talk to me."

He opened the outside door and walked her to the elevator, rode to the second floor with her, then followed her down the hall and into her apartment.

"Please Roman, go back downstairs and let me have today. I'll talk to you tomorrow. I promise I will call you." She walked over to her sofa to sit. Her head was throbbing so she leaned back and closed her eyes.

He did not speak. Instead, he sat next to her and scooped her into his arms, holding her close, not letting her pull away when she tried.

As much as she wanted to protest, she was enjoying being wrapped in his arms. She felt protected from the crazy world and drew strength from him.

Before long she was crying again, overwhelmed by the events of the day and now Roman.

He wiped her tears and rubbed her back, being quiet, not talking, giving her all the time she needed to feel the hurt she was feeling. After a few minutes, she decided to tell him what had her so upset.

Chapter Nineteen

"Twenty five years ago today my son Kendrick died." Lisa was whispering but Roman heard every word. He pulled his arms tighter around her, his mind whirling, trying to remember if she had ever mentioned that she had children. She had not.

"He was in the wrong place at the wrong time and got hit during a gang drive-by. He had been looking for his father at one of the places where he was known to buy drugs. His father was not there. As he was getting in his car to leave the neighborhood, these guys drove up and just started shooting. They killed my son and a couple other people. It broke his father who died soon after from guilt and a drug overdose.

"I'm usually okay and can get through the day without weeping like a heartsick mom. Today is different. Getting to know your wonderful sons over the last few months reminds me of Kendrick. He was about their age when he was killed. I did not want to be at your Mom's place in case they stopped by.

"I went to the cemetery today, first time in a few years. I know he's not there in the crypt anymore, his body became dust long ago, but it makes me feel like I'm close to him just to be there."

She stopped talking when she felt something wet on her face. They weren't her tears this time. They were Romans. She knew then that she couldn't help but fall in love with Roman. How could she not love such a caring heart?

He wiped his face and spoke in her ear.

"I had no idea, and I am so sorry for your loss. Sorry too for not knowing this about you. I can only imagine how you feel, how I would feel. You are so strong to keep this to yourself the way you do. You are an amazing woman."

They sat together with Lisa in his arms for the next half hour. When Lisa went to the bathroom, Roman called Q for food for them and his bag of clothes that he kept in Q's room in case he needed to stay with his Mom in an emergency.

Quincy sent a text when he was on the way and Roman met him at the door. Quincy knew immediately from the look on his brother's face that whatever was happening with Lisa was a crisis and told Roman to let him know when he wanted breakfast, lunch, dinner, and anything else.

Lisa came out of her bathroom ready for bed. Roman had set out the food and encouraged her to eat. She saw his bag by the sofa and looked at him with a question in her eyes.

"Yes, I'm staying here with you tonight, Woman. I keep this bag at Mom's for emergencies."

Lisa did not object. She did not want to be alone tonight even though she tried to be tough and had come home to be by herself. The only person she had ever let stay with her through the storm of her grief was Phyllis, and that was in the early years when the hurt was so fresh. For the last twenty years, her feelings were more manageable so she would just keep herself busy throughout the day.

They ate in relative silence, then she got in bed. He prepared for the night in the guest bathroom, not wanting to use her bathroom until he was invited to do so. When he walked into her bedroom for the first time, he noticed the picture of her and her son on one of the nightstands. As he got in bed with her, he pulled her over to lay her head on his chest.

"Thank you," Lisa whispered, thinking that he was so kind and sincere, more than some other men she had dated. It was a turning point for her when she would no longer deny her feelings for him.

She soon fell into a fitful sleep. Her tears at midnight did not wake her up, but Roman heard her. He wiped her tears, kissed her forehead, and rocked her in his arms until she fell into a deep slumber for the rest of the night.

Chapter Twenty

The next morning, Lisa was feeling better and before they got out of bed, she thanked Roman for being there for her.

"So, I guess you were not going to leave me alone yesterday no matter how many times I asked you to, huh?" She was watching him, seeing him for the compassionate, caring man that he portrayed to her, not just the fun neighbor family guy she was trying to pigeonhole him to be.

"Not when I saw that you were in distress. Other times you might be able to push me away, but I have to help you when you are in need. I didn't know what was wrong, but I knew I needed to be the one to get you through it." He paused to gauge whether he should ask for more information about her son, hoping not to upset her. He took the picture off the nightstand and looked at it while speaking to her.

"Thank you for telling me about Kendrick. I would like to know more about him when you feel up to sharing. If not now, maybe on one of our dates. By the way, do you have any more kids?"

"No, just the one."

"I see. You never talk about your family so I wanted to ask. You are really a private person."

"Not much to tell. I am the baby of three; I have two older brothers. Both parents are deceased. Not a lot of family since both of my parents were only children." She shrugged her shoulders. "I have my share of friends, but I'm pretty much a loner."

"Is that why you try to deny what's happening between us? You don't want to share your life with me?"

"No, I don't mind sharing. I just don't think sharing with you is a good idea."

Roman was quiet for a moment before responding.

"Well, on that sour note, this is going to sound strange, but here's an idea. Let's make our first date today and spend the day out and about together. After all, you have already slept with me. You have to date me now." He gave her a big grin and waited for her response.

Lisa rolled her eyes, then surprised him with her response. "Okay, what do you want to do? Wait, don't you have to work today?"

"I have a conference call at ten then I'm free to hang out with you."

"Okay, but first, I have a question. Why do you call me Woman? Is that how you talk to your lady friends so you don't have to remember their names?"

Roman laughed. "No, Woman. I only call you that. The pronoun is silent."

"What? I don't understand. It's too early in the morning for riddles Roman, so tell me what that means: the pronoun is silent."

"The pronoun is my. It means I am calling you *My Woman* in my mind. I want you to get used to it and know that you are My Woman."

Lisa groaned. "Oh God, Roman. Where did you get that from?"

"It comes from me knowing that I want you. I want us. Knowing that the moment in the elevator was more than a moment and you know that. What? You don't like it?"

"Well you never say my name and it's odd. I never would have picked up on that."

"Well now you know. So, first things first. Good morning, *Lisa*." He rolled over and pressed his lips on hers. She turned her head and scrunched up her nose.

"Ick Roman. Morning breath."

He turned her face back to his, looked her in the eyes, laughing as he responded. "I don't care about yours and you just have to get used to mine."

Before she could respond, he pressed his lips back on hers and paused until he could feel her relax. Her hands began to explore his body. His skin was smooth and his body was tight. Hard inside but soft and warm on the outside.

He pushed her hands off him to stop her. "I want to make love to you in the worst kind of way. Just not today. I don't want to take advantage of you after yesterday and we need to talk about some things first."

"Things like what?" Lisa was feeling vulnerable after yesterday, but she was horny for him too. Was it a form of hero worship? He came to her rescue and now she wanted him?

"Things like you getting rid of Mr. Genesis. What kind of time will you give me so we can be together? Agreeing to an exclusive relationship. Trust me, you will be happy when the time is right. I'm looking forward to hearing you call my name in the heat of passion." The confident smile on his face made her laugh.

"You are so arrogant and bossy! I am an independent woman and I should be able to have what I want. I want you. Now. I am likely to change my mind tomorrow and you will be back in the brother zone." She was hoping her comment would make him change his mind.

Instead, Roman rolled over and laid on top of her. She could feel his hardness pressing between her legs. His left arm slid under her and his right hand caressed her breasts. He began kissing her ear, her cheek, and her neck, whispering,

"This is no brotherly love that I have for you. Be glad I'm a patient man."

Lisa was pleasantly surprised to feel what she felt. He was long and very hard. Her breasts fit perfectly in his hand. Her nipples responded and began to ache as he kneaded them. She gave a soft moan. He did too, in agreement with her that they felt good to each other.

His cell phone alarm went off and his phone rang at the same time, breaking their moment. Roman reluctantly rolled off Lisa and sat up, his back on the headboard, to take the call. Lisa sat up too.

Lisa looked over at him. His eyes were half closed as he rubbed her arm on top of the covers and talked on the phone. He was still hard, and he pushed her hand away when she tried to rub him.

"Q will be here in about twenty minutes with breakfast. My call should take about an hour, then we can go out. Think about what we can do today that will put a smile on your face."

Lisa finally acknowledged to herself that a relationship with Roman could be good. He was thoughtful and kind in addition to being protective. No doubt, he clearly cared about her. Lisa was still frightened that he would end up breaking her heart. Things always start out great, but they change.

Roman could feel Lisa tense up despite his hands rubbing her back. He knew she was closing down on him again but hoped it was just for a moment as she adjusted to them finally taking a giant step toward being together. What else did he need to do to prove himself to her?

Chapter Twenty-One

Their day together was fun. He mentioned at breakfast that he wanted to redo his house when the boys got their own place. Roman had already decided that the boys would share an apartment or Danny's house once they graduated until one of them got married. The boys disagreed and wanted to live with Roman as long as possible.

"I sacrificed my life for them to compensate for the fact that neither of them had a mother in their lives for any length of time. Now I want a woman in my life who can spend nights with me and live with me after we are married. Yes, I do want to get married again. I am sure I will be smarter about it this time around.

"I love my home and it's almost paid for so I would like to keep it. Unless you really don't like it." He was hinting that Lisa would be the one to share his home with him.

She caught the reference and countered, "I don't know if I like it or not. I only saw the family room and bathroom. You should know though, I do not want to live in a two-level house again. I don't want to do stairs as I think about cleaning and aging."

"Okay, we can remedy that. Our first stop today is to tour the house so you can give me ideas on what to do with it to make it sell fast." He saw her eye roll but decided to ignore it. He was on a mission to get her, and he would not be derailed by her skepticism.

"What's next after the house tour?" He wanted this to be a day of her choosing to offset the emotions of the day before.

"There's not a lot to do on a Monday in Houston. Most of the festivals and art shows happen on the weekend. It's the day I run errands.

"How about we go look at model homes? There is a model home park in Iowa Colony. Maybe we can get some ideas from some of the different builders out there. By the time we do that it will be a full day and you can be released back to your life. Your moment saving me from my sorrows will officially be over."

"You are my life now, Woman. By the way, I have decided that you will never be alone again on July 13th. We will be together from the 12th through the 14th each year, and plan something to make a more positive memory each time while honoring Kendrick's life."

"Don't say that Roman. That is a huge commitment. I am just grateful that you were there for me yesterday. I'm good now."

"I see you are still fighting me. That's okay. I'm a fighter too. Let's eat and get dressed. My call won't take long, then we can head out."

The tour of Roman's house was very telling. The whole house was neat and clean. It did not look like three men lived there if men typically being sloppy was the standard. Their décor choices reflected their personalities.

Roman's room was decorated in shades of gray with a navy blue and gray bedcover. Definitely Mr. Conservative.

Eli's walls were metallic silver with red pillows and silver and red striped bed covers. Bold and assertive.

Danny's room was white and black. Very stark.

Danny and Eli were opposites in many ways, but their differences and ability to accept and adjust to one another made for a great bond between them.

The fourth bedroom had a more feminine décor. "These are all leftover from when Mom lived with us," according to Roman.

Throughout the day, Roman introduced her as his wife to the sales people in the model homes. The sales women were professional but very happy to stare at the eye candy walking around. Roman was cordial but unaffected by their attention.

Lisa and Roman talked about cabinet colors and styles, countertops, bathtubs vs showers--all things house related. They even played the "What would you do" game, sharing ideas on how to utilize room space in his house with some of the styles they saw.

Lisa thought Roman would be bored but he was very engaged. He even took pictures of some of the rooms and samples that he thought would work in his house.

Toward the end of the tour, they walked into a one-level open concept house that felt spacious yet cozy, three bedrooms plus an office, staged beautifully with comfortable, contemporary furnishings. When they got about half way through the tour, they looked at each other at the same time and whispered, "This Is It." Roman stopped Lisa in the kitchen and pressed his lips on hers.

Lisa enjoyed being lost in the moments with him. They were both reluctant to say goodbye when they returned to her apartment, but he had to head out of the country on Tuesday for the rest of the week, so he had to get home to pack.

"You need to give Mr. Genesis his notice so that you will be completely free to be with me when I get back."

She did not answer him. He decided that after the fun day they had, combined with his absence, she should be ready to give him her undivided attention. Only time would tell.

Roman made sure they had a long kiss goodbye so they both had something to remember for the time he was away.

He whispered, "The next time I take a trip I want you to go with me. The time of not sleeping together regularly and being apart for days has to end soon, Woman."

"Yes dear." Even Lisa was surprised to hear the words come out of her mouth. But with his tongue in and out of it with such agility, how could she say no? She loved him and was ready to be with him even though she still wanted to ease slowly into the relationship.

She made the call to Ben that she had been putting off. "I've met someone, and I need to give the relationship a real chance. It would not be fair to you to keep going out. I don't date two men at the same time, especially when one might be serious."

Ben was kind and said he understood, but asked, "Is it that guy that's often staring at you when we go out? From that family that's always outside?"

She could not lie. "Yes."

"I had a feeling that it was him. Well, be happy. I will miss you and our dates. See you in church." He hung up sad.

Lisa hung up sorry to have to break up with Ben, but looking forward to what the future would hold with Roman.

Chapter Twenty-Two

Roman sent Lisa flowers on Tuesday then called her every night. He talked to her about everybody in the Thompson family and then details about his work.

"I always travel with a team, a marketing manager, Marcy, and our finance expert, Paul, to cover all aspects of the project. We do feasibility studies for new products, determining how they would fit in the company production system. We have to know the costs associated with the launch, including the proposed costs of any changes we want to recommend, and what the messaging would be for promoting the changes to the Board, our business customers, and the public at-large."

He noticed how much he liked talking with her every day and sharing his life, something he rarely did outside of talking to his brother.

He also learned the details about her parents, which revealed the real reason why she had trust issues, and more about her two older brothers, her deceased husband, and Kendrick since Lisa felt so much better and comfortable sharing with him.

Roman called her from the Los Angeles airport on Friday evening. "I will not get into Houston until long after midnight and I want to see you and sleep with you, but it will be late. I will go home and see you on Saturday."

Lisa said okay, but after they hung up, she decided that she wanted to see him no matter what time he would arrive so she called him back. A female answered in what was clearly her sexy voice.

Lisa could barely speak but she asked for Roman.

"Oh he just went to the bathroom to get ready to board our flight. May I take a message? Who is this?"

"This is Lisa. Who is this?"

"Oh hi! This is Marcy. Are you Ro's sister? I always hear him talking family stuff with you. Nice to meet you. I guess he told you that I travel with him. When he gets an assignment, he makes sure I pack my bags and go too. It's a good life." Marcy laughed softly.

"Anyway, I will tell him to call you but there might not be time since they are calling our section, and he usually goes right to sleep as soon as we get seated."

"Okay. Thanks." Lisa spoke softly into the phone. When she hung up her head was spinning with questions—was there more to Marcy's relationship with Roman, outside of being his marketing manager? Why did she think Lisa was Roman's sister? Clearly, he never told her that he was dating

Lisa. Why was she answering his phone, and in what was surely an after-work voice? Roman said he and Lisa would travel together. Did he mean just on vacations since he had a work girlfriend? Lisa started feeling like she had been played again.

Roman called Lisa on Saturday, several times, but she had turned her phone off. She left it off for the day so that she would not be tempted to check and respond to voice mail or text messages.

He did not go to her apartment because he had promised that he would not intrude on her space just because he could. Quincy said he had not seen her and her car was not in the parking lot. Roman figured he would see her on Sunday, but he had a bad feeling about her silence.

The next day, Lisa was at the counter in the kitchen at Ms. Ruth's cutting cake when Roman walked in. She was determined not to let him interfere with the relationship she had with his Mom and brother. She was just glad that Eli and Danny were not there.

Roman hugged his Mom, fist bumped his brother, then stood behind Lisa, locking his hands on each side of her as he had done at Sugar's. He whispered in her ear, "Hey, Woman. I have called you several times but you have not answered or called me. I missed you. What's going on?"

Lisa never turned around. "Welcome back. Did you want some cake?"

You could feel the heat rising from Roman's body, and just like at Sugar's, not in a good way.

"What I want are answers. Why have we not talked? What is going on? Why are you acting like this? Will you look at me?" He was talking in a low but firm tone in her ear.

"I'll call you later. Right now I need to get Ms. Ruth her cake."

Lisa ducked under his arm with a saucer of cake and a glass of milk and walked over to Ms. Ruth.

When she was about to walk back to the kitchen, Roman intercepted her, taking her arm and moving her rapidly to the patio, closing the door behind them.

He stood with his back to the apartment and Lisa was in front of him so no one could see their facial expressions or hear their conversation.

"Talk to me, Woman. Why are you cutting me off like this? I thought we were good on Friday just before I got on the plane. What happened that you are ignoring my calls and not even reaching out to me?"

Chapter Twenty-Three

Lisa had all day on Saturday and part of Sunday to prepare for this moment. She looked in his eyes and spoke in a clipped tone, reciting facts with no emotion.

"I called you back to ask you to come to me from the airport no matter what time you got in but Marcy answered your phone and said that "Ro" went to the bathroom and would probably fall asleep as usual on the plane so you might not have time to call me back. I guess she did not tell you because you did not call and you did not come over. She thinks I am your sister and let me know that when you travel, you make sure she goes too. I understood that you were not available so I did not bother you."

When she finished she tried to walk around him to go back inside. He cut her off again. He was making a call on his phone with the speaker and recorder on.

"Marcy, this is Roman Thompson." His tone was cold.

"Well hello. This is a nice surprise Ro. What's going on? Should I start packing again?" Her voice was low and sexy.

"It's Roman, not Ro. I have a question for you: did you answer my phone at the airport on Friday evening?"

There was silence on the other end, then a quiet "Yes."

"And who was on that call?"

"Your sister Lisa. I told her that you probably would not have time to call her back then I forgot to tell you. Is everything okay with your family?"

"And did you tell Lisa that we travel together, not like co-workers but as a man and woman in a relationship? Did you tell her that when I get an assignment, I make you pack your bags and go too?"

"Well I do go with you. Just have not been able to cross over to the personal relationship, but I will keep working on it. Did she misunderstand? That's your sister. Why does she care unless something happened in your family?"

"Have I ever talked with you or even hinted to you that I wanted to have a personal relationship with you?"

"No, but I figure it was only a matter of time. You're single, I'm single, we spend a lot of time together on these trips. Why not?"

"The why not is because I am not interested in dating you, plus I do not date people I work with under any circumstance. And for the record, Lisa is not my sister. Far from it. You have crossed the line Marcy. On Monday I am going to get a new marketing manager to go on these trips since you don't know how to keep things professional."

"That's rather drastic. Is all that necessary? Over a forgotten phone call? I am great at what I do for you on these trips. I won't be so easy to replace." Marcy was angry now, seeing her opportunity to be with him disappear and her career being impacted by the change in her not working on the team.

"Everyone is replaceable Marcy. And never touch my phone again." With that, Roman hung up.

Lisa tried again to walk around him but he stopped her, wrapping his arms around her. She stood stiffly with her arms at her side.

"I'm sorry for the misunderstanding. I would have gladly come to you. I wish you had sent me a text or called back when you knew I was in the air and left a message. Can we kiss and make up now? I missed you."

"Thank you for the clarification. I need to get back inside. In fact, it's time for me to head back to my place." Lisa was suddenly tired.

"Here we go again." Roman continued to hold her, sounding disillusioned as he spoke. "Two steps forward, three steps back. First, it was your list and refusal to give up Mr. Genesis. Then Gloria. Now

Marcy. I can't seem to catch a break with you, Woman. Just try to meet me halfway for a change now that you know more about me."

Lisa never responded.

Roman let her walk away and sat down in one of the patio chairs. He knew that Lisa was not pleased with her conversation with Marcy and hoped that when she thought about his call to her, it cleared things up.

He called Lisa to say goodnight before he went to bed but the call went straight to voicemail. His voice message was a warning. "I didn't get my goodnight kiss tonight. I'm coming over tomorrow so you can make it up to me."

When Lisa heard the message, her heart skipped a beat. She wanted to kiss him too. What was the point though?

She agreed with his assessment – two steps forward, three back. Would it ever end?

Chapter Twenty-Four

For the next month, Roman went back to his original plan with Lisa, spending time with her when she was with his family—being friendly, fun, watchful. He still called her every day, even when he went out of town. Most days she answered.

He added walking her home each time she visited with his family so that he could get a few private minutes with her. She would let him in her apartment and he would share his work activities with her and talk about politics, pop culture, and whatever else he could think of to stay with her until it got so late he had to go. He made sure to get a goodnight kiss or two or three.

A couple of times Lisa was tempted to invite him to stay but decided she would not walk herself into the trap with him. He was relentless but did not put a hard press on her. Their friendship was growing so she was more comfortable with him every week. He was slowly seducing her. She knew it and she liked it.

In September, Lisa decided to go to Chicago for a week to spend time with her oldest brother and his family. He had been ill and in and out of hospitals and rehab. She knew he was being well cared for and they talked every week, but she needed to see him for herself.

Roman arranged for her to stay in a hotel for the week on his travel points so she did not have to pay out any money or impose on anyone. He sent her flowers the first day so that her room would smell good and have something to remind her of him. This also gave him freedom to call her in the morning and at night and not disturb anyone else.

The weather in Chicago was unseasonably cold, windy, and rainy. Lisa was not used to it since she had been in Houston for so many years and the weather never got that bad. With so much running around and not being dressed for the weather, she could feel herself getting chills and cold symptoms. She doctored on herself with over-the-counter medicines.

Roman heard a change in her voice and they talked about her going to the doctor while there.

"I'm fine," Lisa assured him though her voice was weak.

"Besides, I will be home tomorrow. I'm staying in the hotel until I leave so that I don't take any germs into my brother's house."

Roman felt better knowing that she would rest. He hesitated about going on his trip, thinking that he needed to look in her face to gauge how she was really doing. The more they talked, though, the more she was able to convince him to go on to Austin for his weeklong business trip.

"I'm taking DayQuil and NyQuil and rubbing my chest with Vicks Vapo-Rub. That should be enough to get me home after I rest tonight. If I don't feel any better once I get home, I'll go to my own doctor."

He left on Sunday, early afternoon. He thought about Lisa not feeling well all during the three-hour drive. More than once he started to turn around, to go back to Houston to her building and wait for her. He finally decided to trust her promise to see her doctor if she was not feeling better when she got home.

Lisa landed late Sunday evening, still feeling bad. She fixed herself some soup and rested in her own bed. It was not enough. Fever developed and coughing started. Throughout the day on Monday, she felt progressively worse. She had chest pains and she could not keep anything on her stomach. She decided to take herself to the emergency room at six o'clock Monday evening.

Quincy saw her leaving and walked over from the patio to her car to ask about her vacation. He knew immediately between the coughing and sweating and the way she was holding her chest that she was not okay.

"I'm taking you to the hospital," he declared.

"No," Lisa whispered. She did not want him to be in a hospital and bring germs back home to his mother so she assured him she would be fine. She told him which hospital emergency room she was going to and promised to call as soon as she was diagnosed.

Quincy ignored her, moving her to his car, then sending a group text to let everyone know that Lisa was sick and he was taking her to Memorial Hermann Hospital Emergency Room on Gessner Road. Eli and Danny knew to check on their Granny when their classes were over. He knew Roman would find out when he finished his business meetings and call for an update.

It was cold and flu season so the emergency room was crowded. Quincy waited with Lisa until they took her back to triage. Lisa insisted he go home and she would text when she had a definitive diagnosis.

They put her in a bed in the emergency room and began to work on her. The two things they knew immediately was that she needed oxygen to help her breathe and her heart rate and urine sample indicated she was dehydrated. It took a couple of hours for them to do the rest of the tests and get the results. With a hydration IV and oxygen mask in place, Lisa was finally able to fall asleep.

Chapter Twenty-Five

When Lisa woke up, the doctor was leaving the room and the nurse was coming in.

"Doctor, do you have some information for me? What is wrong with me? Is it Bronchitis? Pneumonia? What is it? Are you keeping me?"

The doctor stepped back into the room and said, "You have pneumonia. You can go when the nurse turns the oxygen off and takes the IV out." He pointed behind her, "I went over everything with your husband and he said he will make sure you follow the orders."

"Husband?" Lisa sat up and her head snapped around. There sat Roman. One leg was crossed over the other at the knee and he had all of the discharge papers perched there.

This was the first time she had seen him in a business suit, navy blue, with a crisp white shirt and blue and white print tie, black wing-tip shoes. The tie was loose and just hanging around his neck, the collar of his shirt was unbuttoned. He looked especially handsome to Lisa who kept looking him up and down as she got warm and sweaty.

"Hey, Woman," he said with a scowl.

The nurse was looking at him then Lisa then back at him.

Lisa turned back around to look at the nurse as she turned off the oxygen and removed the mask off her face. The nurse was smiling at her.

"I thought you went to Austin yesterday?" Lisa was puzzled.

"I did," he responded.

"Weren't you supposed to be gone all week?"

"I was."

"Were the meetings canceled?"

"No, they were not."

Lisa turned to look at him with a frown on her face. "Then why are you back so soon? Is Ms. Ruth ok? The boys? I saw Quincy so I know he is ok."

"They are all fine."

"Then why are you back so soon? Are you okay?"

"No, I'm not. I'm back because *you are in here, Woman.*" His voice rose to emphasize his concern for her.

The nurse said, "Damn," under her breath and looked at Lisa then Roman again.

The frown relaxed on Lisa's face and she looked him up and down. He could see her fighting a smile, biting her lip.

"Vapors?" He asked with a smile.

"Mm-hmm," Lisa said slowly, pointedly, wiping her face and rubbing her arms.

"Good." He stood up when the nurse said Lisa could get dressed.

The nurse whispered to Lisa, "God is good. Real good!"

Lisa smiled at her and said, "Yes, He is."

"I'll help her." Roman stood over Lisa with her clothes and proceeded to untie the hospital gown.

Lisa tried to stop him, saying she could dress herself.

Roman laughed and whispered to her, "Don't get shy now. I've already seen you undressed and in bed remember?"

"Just go get the car so you can take me home." She wanted a moment alone to think of the magnitude of him leaving his job and driving three hours back to Houston to be with her after a long business day. She was overwhelmed and her heart broke completely open to him and everything he wanted with her.

Lisa was rolled in a wheelchair to the emergency room door just as Roman pulled up in his car. He helped her get in, made sure she was warm, and took her to her place. He had his travel bag with him, so he was prepared to stay with her until she was well.

Roman knew that this was the final turning point he needed to fully claim Lisa as *His Woman*.

Chapter Twenty-Six

For the next three days, Roman made sure Lisa ate, drank plenty of liquids, took her meds on time, took a warm shower, put on fresh sleepwear every night, and got plenty of rest. He ordered groceries for delivery so he could cook for them both, washed their clothes, cleaned the bathrooms and kitchen, and kept up with his business calls.

Lisa slept a lot, but liked the feeling that every time she woke up, he was there. When her energy started to return, she walked out of the bedroom to find him folding clothes and cooking, chicken and vegetable soup for her and some turkey thighs, rice, and Brussel sprouts for himself.

"What all are you doing out here?" She could see he definitely knew his way around a kitchen and the laundry.

"Taking care of you, Woman. What do you need? Do you miss me being in bed with you?" He was licking his lips and winking at her.

"Actually, I do. But I'm afraid that you might get what I have."

He shook his head. "Woman you have coughed and sneezed in my face, laid your sweaty body all over me, snored in my ear, and farted on me. Every night. If I don't have pneumonia by now, I doubt that I will get it."

Lisa hung her head in embarrassment, hands over her face. "Please don't tell me I did all of that on you. I am so sorry. And embarrassed."

"It's all good, as long as you feel better. You see I am still here so it's okay. What is exciting is I get to handle your underwear and see what kind of lingerie you buy. Lots of black and lots of lace. You are a sexy somebody underneath those stylish conservative clothes. This has been most educational. I'm just waiting now for you to get back to normal so you can wear some of these things for me as we consummate this relationship. Just so you know."

"Ohhh. So you think a few days of caregiving will get you some personal privileges with me?"

"Yes, Woman. So get ready. I told you that I was coming for you. Nothing has changed except you are finally opening your mind to us. It's about time you take your rightful place next to me. We belong together and you knew it like I did—as soon as that elevator door opened the first day I met you."

Lisa looked at him but did not respond immediately. Her heart agreed but she refused to admit that yet. She sat at the dining room table. Lunch was ready.

"First day? You really are arrogant."

"Not arrogant. Experienced enough to know what I want when I see it. I saw it in you before I even knew you were the fabulous, fantastic, sexy Lisa Price. I'm just glad the woman in the elevator and Lisa Price turned out to be one and the same."

He plated their food and they ate together for the first time all week. They were both quiet, thinking of what he had just said. When they finished eating, he spoke again.

"I have enjoyed being here with you. Except for your being sick, I'm glad we had this time together."

"Me too," Lisa said quietly. "It's been a long time since any man has taken care of me like this. You are good. Thank you. I appreciate you."

Lisa would not go so far as to confess her love for him. It did not feel like the right time. She would soon enough.

Chapter Twenty-Seven

The next morning, Saturday, Lisa woke up feeling great. No more coughing or sneezing, no fatigue. She was very happy to be feeling healthy and whole again.

Breakfast smelled delicious so before getting dressed she walked out to the kitchen to see what was on the menu.

"It smells like Quincy has been in here working his magic."

Roman stopped stirring in a bowl to set her straight.

"I taught Q how to cook Woman. I am the oldest so I learned first. He caught up quickly though. Never thought he would become a chef! I'm proud of him. He really takes command in any kitchen he is in. But I hold my own."

"Yes, you do. I'm glad because I am not one who wants to be in the kitchen, except for making my desserts. They are fun. You can have all of this other stuff. Too tedious for me."

"Don't worry. I will cook for us. I usually cook two or three days a week anyway when I'm in town. When the boys are on break from school, I take a break too and they cook for me. Now they can cook for us. Breakfast is about ready. Are you hungry?"

"Starving in fact. I will get dressed after I eat. What is on the menu today, Chef Ro-mahn?" She was happy to call him by his fake waiter name, reminding him of his earlier attempts to woo her. He immediately responded in character.

"For your dining pleasure, Beautiful Woman, we have sausage and bacon, oatmeal, soft scrambled eggs, and toast. Did you want anything else?" He was smiling, proud of himself and happy with her surprised reaction.

"Wow. That is more than enough. Thank you!"

As soon as breakfast was over, Lisa cleaned off the table.

"It's the least I can do since you cooked."

She loaded the dishes in the dishwasher, put the leftovers away, got another bottle of water and went back to the table. Roman was sitting in his chair watching her move around the kitchen.

When she sat back down, there was a little square box on the table, open in front of Lisa so she could see the ring inside. When she saw it, she looked startled then looked up at Roman. He was looking at her with his usual amused smile in his eyes and his upturned mouth.

"I like you, Woman. I have liked your spirit and your heart since I first started hearing the wonderful stories about you from all of the people who are important to me. Now that I have come to know you for myself, I can admit I like you too. In fact, I have grown to love you.

"I told you before you bring something to my life that I did not know I was missing: a calmness and sense of peace. Your presence makes me better on my job, you make being a father more manageable, and thinking about my aging Mother and something happening to her less stressful. Not sure if my family can tell that I am more relaxed, but it feels like a weight has been lifted. Someone on my job noticed though, and remarked the other day that I seemed different lately, not as stressed in meetings and less agitated when something goes wrong.

"Every time I am around you, I feel better. The weird thing is I feel safe around you too. You have such a caring soul that I feel protected with you, that you will not let anyone hurt me. That is unusual for a man to feel with a woman. At least for me it is. I grew up under Charles Thompson who said the man is always the protector.

"I am in love with you Ms. Lisa Price. Totally and completely. Until death do us part love.

"So today, I am asking you to marry me. Share my life, let me be fully involved in yours. Let me take care of you every day, not just when you are sick. Take care of me in the way only you can. Be a mother to my sons. Even though they are adults, they still need mothering and they love you. They want you to be the mother they never had.

"Let's have some fun together, make travel plans, and make love...whatever your heart and that sexy body of yours desires." He stopped talking and waited for her to respond.

Lisa stared at him for a full minute before responding.

"Wow. Those are powerful words, Roman. Beautiful, romantic, sexy. Thank you. I love you too." They looked at each other in recognition that this was the beginning of their lives sealed together.

As she looked at him, her facial expression changed, going from soft and loving to questioning to smiling to devilish as she looked at him.

"But are you sure we are ready for marriage? We have only had one real date. We have not, ugh, as you say, consummated the relationship either. How do we know that we are compatible? What if there is nothing behind the vapors? I don't want you to be disappointed. And I don't want to be either."

Lisa blushed when she said it, but sexual compatibility was important. The vapors were no guarantee that they would be good together. Lisa needed to know that they would be so dates and sex were required, at least for her to make such a commitment.

Chapter Twenty-Eight

Roman laughed, surprising Lisa. "We have been dating every time we see each other. We talk about everything, we have shared movies, jokes, personal histories, sad times, illness; it just hasn't been outside of this building too much. I don't know how much more you would get to know about me if we did go out.

"We will date after we get married. We will have date nights in town and out of town, every week or two, and you can have your pick of things for us to do. Will that work for you?"

Lisa slowly shook her head yes.

"As for sexual compatibility...now I'm shocked. You are one naughty lady under all of that class. That's okay. I tell you what. I'll audition for you. I am sure I will be better than those toys in your nightstand. If I hear any sounds of satisfaction, then you have to take the ring. Deal?"

It was Lisa's turn to laugh. He had turned the tables on her so smoothly all she could do was nod in agreement.

"Okay, with that settled, what shall we do today? Want to watch a movie? I think you need one more day in before you get back to your schedule."

Roman was ready to move away from the table but not ready to go out into the world just yet.

"Since this is a day of romance, let's binge watch that new series, *Leap of Faith*. It is on Netflix, or Lifetime, or the Hallmark channel. I can't remember which one. First, let me jump in the shower. I'll be ready in ten minutes."

Lisa brushed her teeth, washed her face, and stepped into a nice warm shower. Just as she put her favorite gel on her towel, Roman stepped in behind her and took the towel from her. He wrapped his left arm around her to hold her close and used his right arm to slowly put soap on each breast, her navel, and her hips. He opened her legs with his knee so he could reach down and stroke inside her with the towel and then his fingers, all the while kissing her ear, neck, and back.

Lisa was very pleasantly surprised at Roman coming into the shower. Her breasts felt like they were swelling to fill his hands, and her nipples responded to Roman squeezing them. The vapors were back and strong.

He turned her around and kissed her as she put soap all over him too. They rinsed off and stepped out of the shower. He dried her off and used the same towel for himself then led her to the bed.

They kissed with a new hunger for one another, lips sealed together and tongues refusing to break away. Roman leaned back so he could reach under Lisa's hips and raise her up where he could slide inside her in one slow, throbbing movement. Once inside her, he leaned forward and gathered her in his arms.

Lisa's face was in his chest so he couldn't see her but he heard her moan then call out his name. She licked and sucked his nipples while gently kissing his chest and rubbing his back. He moaned too. They found a gentle yet urgent rhythm for their first mating dance.

Roman whispered something very naughty in her ear to tell her how much he was enjoying her body, her hands, her lips, and her tongue. He needed to know how she would respond to that side of him.

She responded with something very naughty in his ear, which made him increase his tempo inside her body and tell her how much he loved her.

Their first orgasms were strong and long, leaving them both winded and sweaty.

Roman got up first and placed a sheet over Lisa's body so she would not get cold. Her eyes followed him, admiring his body and replaying in her mind what they had just done.

When she came out of the bathroom, he was in bed, flat on his back, arms behind his head, legs crossed at the ankle, with the ring box sitting open on top of his stomach.

The engagement ring had three Marquise diamonds set in platinum. The wedding band had Pave diamonds all around it.

Roman explained, "The boys helped me design the engagement ring so that it has diamonds representing all three sons: Kendrick, Eli, Danny. The band is my part, a solid circle of my love. I hope you like it."

His look was hopeful, and he patiently waited for her to respond. She was looking at him with such love and adoration that his heart grew full. She was overwhelmed and bit her lip to keep from letting tears fall. She shook her head yes then held up her left hand. He slid the engagement ring on. A perfect fit.

Chapter Twenty-Nine

They spent the rest of the day in bed, talking, kissing, and making love.

Roman asked, "When will you be ready to get married? I have no desire to wait, just so you know."

Lisa was ready too. She had a big wedding the first time and that was enough.

"Let's get the license on Monday and if the family and Phyllis can make it, we can just get married at the courthouse on Friday. We need to do it after the 72 hour waiting period."

Roman was very happy to hear that.

They talked about her moving to his house with him and his sons. She grew up around her two older brothers so she was comfortable with the idea of being in the house with the three men, but what would they do with her furniture?

Roman had a suggestion. "How about we clear out the fourth bedroom so you can have the space for whatever you want to keep. Anything left over, we will find room or get rid of it."

She was happy with that.

He sent a message through the family text to let them know that she said "yes" and told the boys they had to be at his Mom's house on Sunday for dinner.

When they walked into Ms. Ruth's on Sunday afternoon, Roman and Lisa were glowing from love and lots of sex that kept them in bed until an hour before they went down to be with the family. Lisa ordered Tiff's Treats cookies for delivery because there was no time to bake.

The family was talking until the door opened. Roman walked through first grinning and fist pumping the air, then held the door open for Lisa to walk through.

Roman's sons cheered and immediately went over to hug her. Danny asked when they could start calling her Mom and Lisa quickly responded, "Anytime you feel comfortable."

Eli wanted to know when she was moving into their family home.

"As soon as you guys can get me packed." Lisa was happy to report. They promised to get boxes and tape and pack her up the following weekend. They were eager to have her move to the house with them.

Quincy gave his brother a big hug and whispered in his ear, "Finally! You did good, man. Congratulations."

He then gave Lisa a big hug and officially welcomed her to the family. "Now you are my sister for real. I could not be happier."

The engaged couple finally got to Ms. Ruth who was standing by the sofa crying. She hugged Roman and said, "I have not seen you this happy in a long, long time. I'm glad I lived to see it."

She held Lisa close so she could whisper in her ear. "I see you like getting touched by a Thompson. The acorn must have made his daddy proud. You said yes."

Lisa could only laugh and say, "He did. So of course I had to say yes."

"Good. I can die a happy woman now knowing all of my family is in your very warm caring hands. No more Ms. Ruth for you. It's Mom. Thank you for loving my family and me and making us all so very happy by saying yes to my son. I love you, my daughter."

"Thank you for having such a wonderful son and raising him to be a magnificent man, Mom." They hugged until the guys started clamoring for information on wedding plans.

"We have no desire to wait so we are going tomorrow to get the license. If you and Lisa's friend Phyllis are all available to come with us, we will get married there too, on Friday."

They all said yes, and Lisa put in a quick call to Phyllis who was thrilled to say she was definitely available.

Lisa teased Roman. "I guess I should give Ben his notice now since I can't see him on Friday's anymore."

Roman shook his head. "Woman, you did that after we spent the first night together and the next day at the model homes. Don't try to play me."

"How do you know that was when?"

"Because I have deliberately taken up your time every Friday night ever since. I had a plan for you Woman. I told you I was coming for you. I studied you. I knew when the plan was working. I'm just very happy that you are now ready for our life together to begin."

Lisa was ready to live with Roman with complete trust, no hesitation, and no regrets. Roman committed to giving her the vapors at least once a month.

# # #

ABOUT THE AUTHOR

PAM KELLY spent her teen years on Chicago's South Side reading romance novels and watching her parents live out their own real life love story. After earning two master's degrees and having a successful career in advertising, she went from studying brands to studying the magic and nuance of relationships – her own and others -- and now writes about them in sensual romance novels. Her characters are bold and strong, flawed and sensitive, and all kinds of sexy. Their stories are compelling, heart wrenching, and romantic.

Pam loves reading, music, organizing and decorating, a good laugh, and beautiful shoes. Her Goddaughters and nieces and their children keep her busy and up-to-date on all things new. She resides in Houston, Texas.

Connect with Pam online and in social media:
    *AuthorPamKelly.com
    ptFacebook: Author Pam Kelly
    Instagram: AuthorPamKelly
    TikTok: AuthorPamKelly

www.ingramcontent.com/pod-product-compliance
Lightning Source LLC
Chambersburg PA
CBHW051951290426
44110CB00015B/2195